W9-BZN-269

THE CHOCOLATE COOKBOOK

THE CHOCOLATE COOKBOOK

ELIZABETH WOLF COHEN

Crescent Books
New York/Avenel, New Jersey

A QUINTET BOOK

This 1992 edition published by
Crescent Books, distributed by
Outlet Book Company Inc.
a Random House Company
40 Engelhard Avenue, Avenel, New Jersey 07001

ISBN 0-517-07315-3

8 7 6 5 4 3 2 1

This book was designed and produced by
Quintet Publishing Limited
6 Blundell Street
London N7 9BH

Project Editor: Laura Sandelson
Creative Director: Richard Dewing
Designer: Stuart Walden
Editor: Beverly Le Blanc
Photographer: Nelson Hargreaves
Home Economists: Pamela Westland, Suzanne Ardley

Typeset in Great Britain by
Central Southern Typesetters, Eastbourne
Manufactured in Hong Kong by
Regent Publishing Services Limited
Printed in Hong Kong by
Leefung-Asco Printers Limited

ACKNOWLEDGMENT
The publishers would like to thank Cadbury Ltd, Bournville, England, for supplying chocolate and cocoa used in the preparation of the recipes.

Table of contents

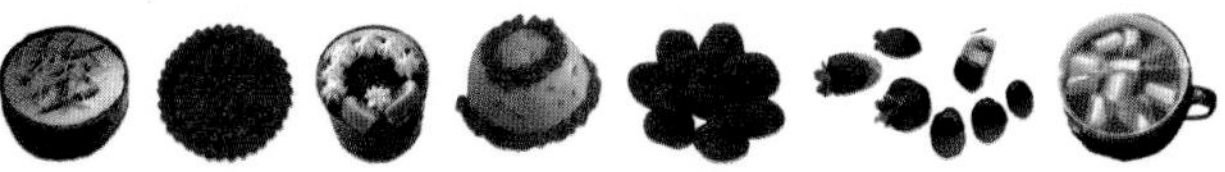

Introduction

1 Semisweet chocolate
2 Imported bittersweet
3 Baker's chocolate (unsweetened)
4 Imported milk chocolate
5 Milk chocolate
6 Cocoa
7 White chocolate
8 Imported bittersweet
9 Milk chocolate

TYPES OF CHOCOLATE

Chocolate can be found in many forms from solid to premelted, from extra dark to white, from unsweetened to sweet and milky. In its powdered form, chocolate is cocoa powder. All chocolate, even those of the same type, tastes different depending on the quality and roasting of the beans, the quality and style of production and the national tastes of the country in which the chocolate is manufactured.

Both eating and cooking chocolate are made from chocolate liquor, which is blended with additional cocoa butter, sugar and flavorings. The more chocolate liquor and cocoa butter the chocolate contains, the higher the quality. Each country of production has certain minimum standards. Although certain chocolate lends itself to particular preparations, chocolate is very much a personal preference.

UNSWEETENED CHOCOLATE

Also known as Baker's chocolate, or bitter chocolate (not bittersweet), unsweetened chocolate is the cooled chocolate liquor with a quantity of cocoa butter reblended. It has a bitter, intense, full chocolate flavor and is used mainly in manufacturing chocolate products. If unable to find it in a store, an adequate substitution for 1 square (1 oz.) unsweetened chocolate for baking is 3 tbsp. (¾ oz.) cocoa powder, plus 1 tbsp. unsalted butter. The sugar in the recipe must then also be adjusted.

SEMISWEET OR BITTERSWEET CHOCOLATE

This type of chocolate varies from extra bittersweet, to bittersweet, to semisweet. This chocolate contains only chocolate liquor, cocoa butter and sometimes lecithin (an emulsifier) and sugar in varying quantities, as well as sometimes vanilla. Each country has varying guidelines for the contents of cocoa solids which accounts for the broad variety of quality. In the U.S, this chocolate must contain 34 percent solids, and in Great Britain, 35 percent. Best results in cooking are obtained with chocolate which contains a minimum of 50 percent chocolate solids. Although interchangeable in recipes, use a more bitter chocolate if you prefer a less sweet flavor.

MILK CHOCOLATE

In 1875, Daniel Peter succeeded in adding condensed milk to chocolate liquor which produced the first milk chocolate. Nowadays, milk chocolate is made most commonly with dried milk powder. It has a much milder flavor than dark chocolate and cannot be substituted for bittersweet or dark chocolate in baking and dessert recipes because it has a lower cocoa solid content. Milk chocolate scorches easily when melting, so take care.

WHITE CHOCOLATE

Technically, white chocolate is not chocolate at all because it does not contain any chocolate liquor. It is a commercial product made from cocoa butter, milk and sugar. In the U.S., it is called a confectionery coating, and some white chocolate may contain vegetable fat as well as, or instead of, cocoa butter, so read the label carefully. White chocolate has been gaining in popularity recently and is used in mousses, cakes and sauces, and to contrast in color with other chocolates. As with milk chocolate, it is more sensitive to heat, so be very careful when melting it. Use a water-bath or "bain marie" and keep the temperature between 110°F and 120°F.

COUVERTURE OR COVERING CHOCOLATE

This is a very fine, richly flavored chocolate with a glossy appearance and smooth texture because of the high proportion of cocoa butter it contains. It is expensive and mostly used by professionals for coating and dipping other chocolates. This chocolate must be tempered (p8). It is available in some specialty stores or by mail order (in the U.S.) as bittersweet, semisweet, milk or white. Although it can be used when a very fine flavor and texture are required, it is not generally used in baking or dessert making.

Do not confuse couverture with commercial coating chocolate or cake covering, made with the addition of other fats and oils, which is cheaper and easier to use but lacks the flavor and gloss of fine couverture.

CHOCOLATE CHIPS

Originally produced by chocolate manufacturers in the U.S. for use in chocolate chip cookies, these pieces are now available as mini-, regular-, or maxi-sized and as bittersweet, semi-sweet, milk and white. Because they were designed to keep their shape in a variety of baked goods, they are best used in recipes like cookies, cakes and confections where their shape adds extra texture or interest. Although they can be melted, they contain less cocoa butter than ordinary chocolate.

COCOA POWDER

Cocoa powder is the pure chocolate mass which is left when some of the cocoa butter is removed from the chocolate liquor. Ground and sifted, this powder gives the most intense chocolate flavor to baked goods and desserts.

Dutch-process cocoa or Dutch cocoa is neutralized by a process called "Dutching," giving the cocoa a darker, reddish color but a slightly milder flavor. This is sometimes called European-style cocoa, as almost all imported cocoas are made by the Dutch process.

Nonalkalized cocoa powder most commonly available in the U.S. has a sharper more robust flavor because the acids are left untreated. Unless specified they can be used interchangeably, although the flavor of "natural" cocoa powder is more intense. In baking, cocoa should be sifted into other dry ingredients or diluted with boiling water to form a paste, much like cornstarch, before being added to other mixtures.

Drinking chocolate is a commercial preparation with added sugar and sometimes dried milk solids.

COOKING WITH CHOCOLATE

Chocolate must be treated very carefully. The single most important technique to be mastered in cooking with chocolate is melting it. There are several ways to melt chocolate, but there are only a few basic rules to follow for successful results.

If chocolate is being melted on its own, all the equipment and utensils involved must be *perfectly dry*, as even a single drop of water may cause the chocolate to "block," that is, thicken and become a stiff, unworkable paste. For this reason, do not cover the pan at any time during or after melting chocolate. If chocolate does block while being melted alone, try adding a little vegetable shortening (not butter or margarine as these both contain water) and mix well. If this does not work, start again. Do not discard the chocolate, it may be used in a recipe which melts the chocolate in another liquid.

Chocolate can be melted with a liquid, if there is enough liquid. If melted with butter, cream, milk, water, coffee or a liqueur, it is less likely to burn. Generally 1 tbsp. liquid to each 2 squares (2 oz.) chocolate should be safe, but if the chocolate appears to be thickening, add a little more liquid.

With or without liquid, chocolate should be melted *very slowly*. It is very easily burned or scorched, and overheated chocolate can turn gritty and develop a poor flavor. Whatever the method used, chocolate should not be heated above 120°F; milk and white chocolate should not be heated above 110°F. Remember this will feel *warm* not hot as normal body temperature is 98.6°F. If chocolate is broken up into small pieces it will melt smoothly and quickly.

DOUBLE BOILER METHOD

This is probably the most traditional method for melting chocolate. If you do not have a double boiler, create one by placing a small heatproof bowl over a saucepan. Make sure the bowl fits snugly so none of the water or steam can splash into the bowl. Leave the water in the bottom of the double boiler or pan to come to a boil, then place the chocolate, broken into small pieces or chopped, into the double boiler top or bowl and place on double boiler bottom or saucepan. Lower the heat or turn it off completely and allow the chocolate to melt slowly, stirring frequently until smooth.

SAUCEPAN METHOD (DIRECT HEAT)

When chocolate is melted with a liquid such as milk, cream or even butter, it can be melted over direct heat in a saucepan. Choose a heavy-bottomed saucepan and melt the chocolate over low heat, stirring frequently until it is melted and smooth. Remove from heat immediately. This method is also used for making sauces, frostings and some candies.

Chocolate can also be melted in a very low oven (225°F or less). Place the chocolate in an ovenproof bowl and heat in the oven for a few minutes. Remove the chocolate before it is completely melted and stir until smooth.

MICROWAVE METHOD

The microwave is an ideal tool for melting chocolate quickly and easily. The chopped or broken chocolate should be placed in a microwave-safe bowl and cooked on Medium power (50%) about 2 minutes for 4 squares (4 oz.) bittersweet or semisweet chocolate. Milk and white chocolate should be melted on Low power (30%) for about 3 minutes for 4 squares (4 oz.) chocolate. (These times are for a 650w to 700w oven.) These are *approximate* times and both chocolate and microwave ovens vary, so check the chocolate halfway through cooking time. The chocolate does not change shape, but begins to look shiny and must then be stirred until melted and smooth. *Take care;* chocolate can burn in the microwave so be sure to check frequently and continue to microwave at 5- to 10-second intervals if chocolate is not melted enough.

Chocolate melted with liquid or butter may melt more quickly if the liquid has a high-fat content, so check the time carefully.

TEMPERING CHOCOLATE

Tempering is a process of slowly heating and cooling chocolate to stabilize the emulsification of cocoa solids and butter fat. This technique is generally used by professionals with couverture chocolate, which allows chocolate to shrink quickly (for easy release from a mold) or to be kept at room temperature for several weeks or months without loosing its crispness and shiny surface. All solid chocolate is tempered in production, but once melted it loses its "temper" and must be retempered unless it is to be used immediately.

Untempered chocolate tends to "bloom," that is, becomes dull and streaky or takes on a cloudy appearance, but this can be avoided if melted chocolate is refrigerated immediately. General baking and dessert making does not require tempering, which is a relatively fiddly procedure and takes practice and experience. It is, however, used to prepare the chocolate before making many sophisticated decorations such as Chocolate Curls and Scrolls (see Decorating in Chocolate). These shapes and decorations can easily be made without tempering chocolate if they are refrigerated immediately and stored in the refrigerator. Basically, chilling the chocolate solidifies the cocoa butter and prevents it from rising to the surface or "blooming."

Couverture chocolate is usually used for coating because its high butterfat content means it melts to a fluid and beautiful coating consistency. Tempering requires a thermometer (preferably an instant read). Melt the chocolate in the top of a double boiler by heating it to 100° to 115°F, stirring frequently. Remove the top of the double boiler and set in a pan or bowl of cold water to cool chocolate to 80° to 82°F, stirring constantly. Return the top of the double boiler to the heat and reheat the chocolate to 86° to 91°F for dark chocolates, from

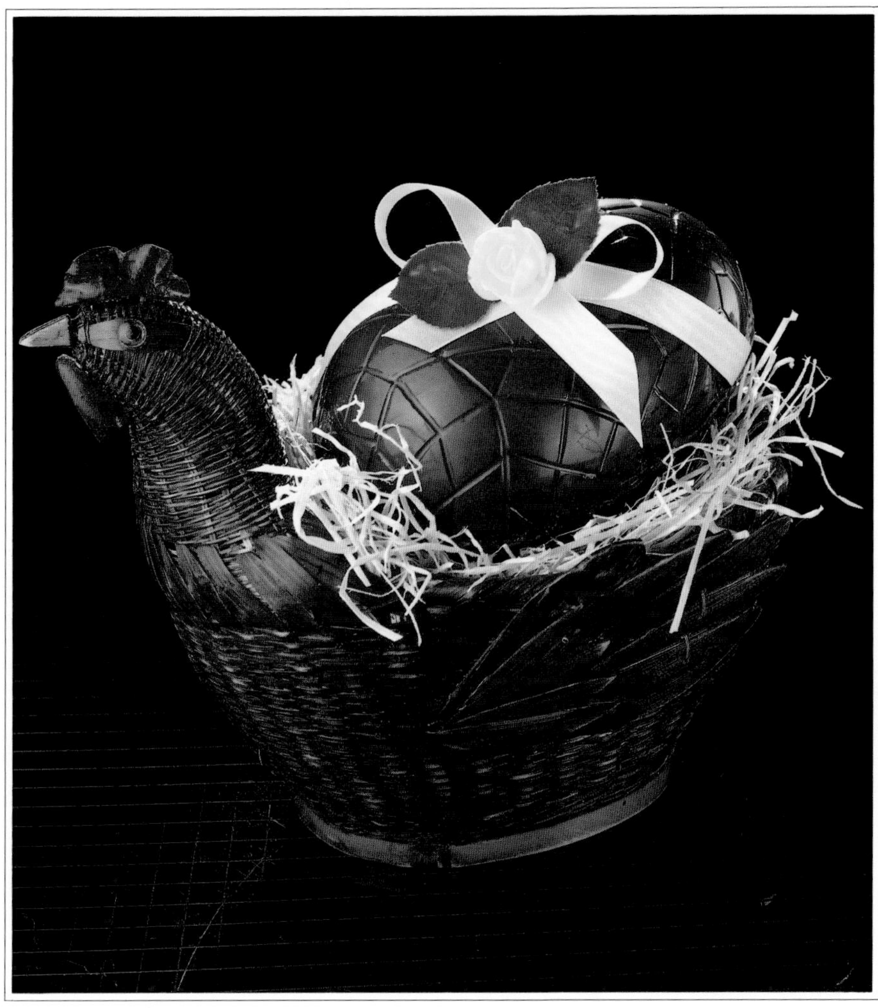

84° to 88°F for milk chocolate and from 84° to 86°F for white chocolate. The chocolate must be maintained at this temperature, setting the double boiler top in a bowl of warm water or on a heating pad. Any leftover chocolate can be used again but if melted down, will require tempering.

CHOCOLATE FOR COATING

Truffles, caramels and other candies, as well as fresh or dried fruit pieces, can all be coated in chocolate. The tempered couverture chocolate described above is the ideal method, but melted bittersweet or semisweet chocolate can be used if the chocolate is refrigerated immediately.

Melt the chocolate by the preferred method, then pour into a bowl deep enough to cover whatever is being coated. The temperature should be between 110° and 120°F but never above that. Use a fondue fork, skewer or special chocolate dipping fork to lower the candy into the chocolate. Turn to coat, and lift out of the melted chocolate, tapping gently on the edge of the bowl to remove excess chocolate. Place on a waxed paper-lined cookie sheet, and, if you like, draw tines of fork across the top, lifting lightly to leave two raised ridges.

MOLDING CHOCOLATE

Making Easter eggs and chocolate bunnies or Santas is easy to do at home. There are many especially shaped molds available in metal and plastic; plastic is easier to use and allows the beginner to see when the chocolate has set and shrunk. The molds must be immaculately clean; do not use abrasive materials to clean any mold as even the slightest scratch may cause the chocolate to stick.

Melt and temper couverture or bittersweet or semisweet chocolate as described above (large molds may need several layers of chocolate), and pour into the mold, tilting the mold and swirling the chocolate so the mold is completely coated; turn out any excess chocolate. Place mold upside down on a waxed paper-lined cookie sheet and allow to set until firm. Repeat if necessary and then allow chocolate to set until hard and chocolate begins to shrink away from the edge of the mold. Gently shake the shape out of the mold, without touching it (this would leave fingerprints) onto waxed paper. Use melted chocolate as "glue" to stick together two halves of shapes like Easter eggs and other figures. Tie larger molds with ribbon or decorate with white frosting to give as presents.

DECORATING WITH CHOCOLATE

Chocolate makes an ideal garnish for most desserts and cakes, even those which are not made with chocolate. Some are very simple to make, while others require more skill and patience. It is worth making most chocolate garnishes in quantity, as they can be stored for several weeks in an airtight container in the refrigerator depending on whether the chocolate is tempered or not (see page 8).

GRATED CHOCOLATE

Chill the chocolate and hold it with a piece of foil to prevent the heat of your hand melting it. Hold a hand or box grater over a large bowl and grate the amount of chocolate required. A food processor fitted with the metal blade can also be used to grate chocolate, *but* be sure the chocolate is soft enough to be pierced with a sharp knife. Cut the chocolate into small pieces and with the machine running, drop the chocolate pieces through the feed tube until grated (this produces very fine shavings).

EASY CHOCOLATE CURLS

Bring a thick piece or bar of chocolate to room temperature (too cold the chocolate will "grate" and too warm it will slice). With a swivel-bladed vegetable peeler held over a cookie sheet or plate, draw the blade along the edge of the chocolate, letting curls fall onto the cookie sheet in a single layer. Use a skewer or toothpick to transfer them to the dessert or cake because your fingers will melt the curls.

LONG CHOCOLATE CURLS

These curls are best made with dark chocolate which is melted with vegetable fat (about 1 tsp. per 1 square (1 oz.) chocolate keeps the chocolate slightly malleable). Melt 6 squares (6 oz.) bittersweet or semisweet chocolate with 2 tbsp. vegetable fat or shortening, stirring until smooth. Pour into a small, foil-lined rectangular or square pan to produce a 1-in.-thick block. Refrigerate until set. Leave the block to come to room temperature. Use a box grater to produce long curls or a swivel-bladed vegetable peeler for shorter rounder curls.

SCROLLS OR SHORT ROUND CURLS

Melted dark or white chocolate, tempered chocolate or chocolate prepared for Long Chocolate Curls (p10) can be used to produce these scrolls. Prepare the melted chocolate and pour onto a marble slab or onto the back of a cookie sheet; with a metal spatula, spread to about ⅛-in. thick and leave to set until firm, about 30 minutes.

To make long scrolls, use the blade of a long, sharp knife on the surface of the chocolate and both hands to push away from your body at a 45° angle to scrape off a thin layer of chocolate. Twist the handle of the knife one-quarter of a circle to produce a slightly cone-shaped scroll. To make shorter round curls with a rounder shape, use a teaspoon to scrape chocolate away.

A variety of shapes and sizes can be produced, depending on the temperature of the chocolate and the utensil used to scrape the chocolate into curls. Knives, metal spatulas, paint scrapers, teaspoons, tablespoons and even wide, straight, pastry scrapers can be used. The colder the chocolate the more it will splinter; warmer chocolate gives a softer looser curl, but do not let the chocolate become too soft or warm or it will be too difficult to handle or may begin to bloom.

A marbled effect can be achieved by pouring about 1 square (1 oz.) melted chocolate of a contrasting color over the back of cookie sheet in a swirling pattern, then pouring over the melted chocolate of the main color and spreading it as directed. When scraped off it will have a marbled effect.

CHOCOLATE SHAPES

Prepare melted chocolate, but pour onto a waxed paper-lined cookie sheet and spread evenly to about ⅛-in. thick. Leave to cool until firm, at least 30 minutes. Invert the chocolate onto another sheet of waxed paper and, with a knife, trim edges to make a perfect rectangle. Using a ruler, mark even squares, rectangles or diamond shapes and then cut out with a knife. Alternatively, use cookie cutters or aspic cutters to make decorative shapes. Use a plain pastry tip to punch a hole in the top and thread with a ribbon for ornaments or use a contrasting chocolate to decorate with another design or write names on the surface.

A marbled effect can be achieved by swirling in a small amount of a contrasting chocolate color (about 1 square to 6 squares) to the main color and allowing it to set before cutting out shapes.

CHOCOLATE LEAVES

Any fresh, non-toxic leaf with distinct veins, such as rose, bay or lemon leaves, can be used. Wash and dry leaves thoroughly. Melt the chocolate and use a pastry brush or spoon to completely coat each veined side of leaf. Place coated leaves chocolate-side up on a waxed paper-lined cookie sheet to set. Starting at the stem end, gently peel away leaf and return chocolate leaves to waxed paper until ready to use.

DRIZZLED CHOCOLATE

Melt chocolate and spoon into a paper cone (see below) or small pastry bag fitted with a very small plain tip. Drizzle chocolate onto a waxed paper-lined cookie sheet in small, self-contained lattice shapes, such as circles or squares, then leave to set until firm, about 30 minutes, before peeling off paper.

Chocolate can be piped in many designs, such as flowers or butterflies. Place a sheet of waxed paper over a chosen design and pipe chocolate, tracing over the design or shape as a guide. Pull paper over design for each tracing.

For butterflies, pipe chocolate onto individually cut squares and leave until just beginning to set. Use an egg carton or empty box of foil or plastic wrap and place the butterfly shapes between the cups or onto box so it is bent in the center, creating the butterfly shape. Chill until ready to use.

CHOCOLATE CUPS

Regular cupcake liners or candy cases can be used to make small or mini-chocolate cases to fill with ice creams, mousses, puddings or other dessert mixtures. Use double liners inside each other for extra support. Melt dark, milk or white chocolate and, using a spoon or pastry brush, completely coat the bottom and side of the case. Leave to set, then add a second layer of melted chocolate. Leave to set overnight or at least 5 to 6 hours. Carefully peel off cupcake liner or candy case.

MAKING A PAPER CONE

A paper cone is ideal for piping small amounts of messy liquids like melted chocolate because they are small and easy to handle and can be thrown away; this avoids cleaning a pastry bag. Fold a square of waxed paper or parchment paper in half to form a triangle. With triangle point facing you, fold left corner down to center. Fold right corner down and wrap completely around folded left corner, forming a cone. Fold ends into cone. Spoon liquid into cone and fold top edges over to enclose filling. When ready to pipe, snip off end of point to make a hole about ⅛ in. in diameter.

Cakes

CLASSIC DEVIL'S FOOD CAKE

CHOCOLATE-CHESTNUT ROULADE

CHOCOLATE ANGEL CAKE

MARBLED CHOCOLATE-PEANUT BUTTER BUNDT CAKE

CHOCOLATE-SOUR CREAM CAKE

SAUCY CHOCOLATE CAKE

CHOCOLATE-MINT CUPCAKES

BITTERSWEET CHOCOLATE-PECAN TORTE

WHITE CHOCOLATE AND COCONUT LAYER CAKE

EASY CHOCOLATE TRUFFLE CAKE

BLACKOUT CAKE

CHOCOLATE-RASPBERRY TORTE

BLACK FOREST CAKE

CHOCOLATE-BANANA SWIRL CHEESECAKE

WHITE CHOCOLATE CHEESECAKE

TRIPLE CHOCOLATE CHEESECAKE

CLASSIC DEVIL'S FOOD CAKE

10–12 SERVINGS

This is a rich, dark chocolate layer cake with a reddish tint which comes from the cocoa powder. It is filled and frosted with a smooth chocolate ganache frosting – a chocolate lover's dream cake.

2 squares (2 oz.) unsweetened chocolate, chopped
1/4 cup unsweetened cocoa powder
2 1/4 cups cake flour
2 tsp. baking soda
1/2 tsp. salt
1/2 cup (1 stick) unsalted butter, softened
2 1/2 cups packed soft brown sugar
1 tbsp. vanilla extract
3 eggs
3/4 cup sour cream (or buttermilk)
1 tsp. vinegar
1 cup boiling water

CHOCOLATE GANACHE FROSTING
3 cups whipping cream
24 squares (1 1/2 lbs.) bittersweet or semisweet chocolate, chopped
1 tbsp. vanilla extract

Preheat oven to 375°F. Butter two 9-in. cake pans. Line bottoms with waxed paper; butter paper and flour pans.

In the top of a double boiler over low heat, melt chocolate, stirring frequently until smooth. Set aside. Sift together cocoa powder, cake flour, baking soda and salt.

With electric mixer, cream butter, brown sugar and vanilla until light and creamy, about 5 minutes, scraping side of bowl occasionally. Add eggs 1 at a time, beating well after each addition.

Add flour mixture alternately with sour cream in 3 batches, beating until well blended. Stir in vinegar and slowly beat in boiling water; batter will be thin. Pour into pans.

Bake 20 to 25 minutes, until cake tester inserted in center comes out with just a few crumbs attached. Cool cakes in pans on wire rack. Remove cakes from pans and paper and cool on wire rack while preparing frosting.

In a saucepan over medium heat, bring cream to a boil. Remove from heat and stir in chocolate all at once until melted and smooth. Cool slightly. Pour into large bowl and refrigerate 1 hour, stirring twice, until frosting is spreadable.

With serrated knife, slice each cake layer horizontally into 2 layers. Place 1 cake layer cut-side up on cake plate and spread with one-sixth of the frosting. Place second layer on top and frost with another sixth of the frosting. Place a third layer on top and cover with another sixth of the frosting, then cover with fourth cake layer top-side (rounded) up. Frost top and side of cake with remaining frosting. Serve at room temperature.

SWEET SUCCESS

Cake layers can be made several days ahead, wrapped tightly in plastic wrap and stored in the refrigerator. Bring to room temperature before frosting. Ganache frosting should be used when it reaches spreading consistency.

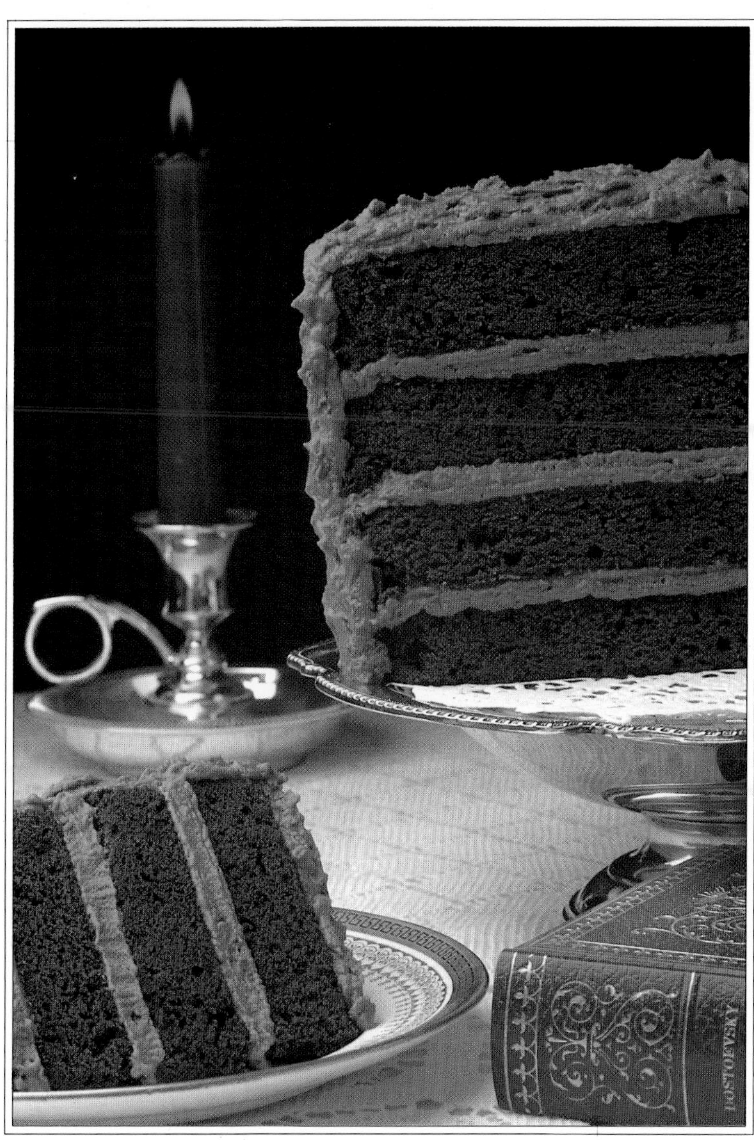

CHOCOLATE-CHESTNUT ROULADE

12 SERVINGS

This combination of a dark chocolate sponge and chestnut flavored cream is an elegant one.

6 squares (6 oz.) semisweet chocolate, chopped
¼ cup strong coffee
6 eggs, separated
6 tbsp. superfine sugar
½ tsp. cream of tartar
2 tsp. vanilla extract
cocoa powder for dusting

CHESTNUT CREAM FILLING
2 cups heavy cream
2 tbsp. coffee-flavor liqueur *or* 2 tsp. vanilla extract
2 cups canned sweetened chestnut purée
confectioners' sugar
candied chestnuts for garnish

Preheat oven to 350°F. Grease bottom and sides of 15½- × 10½- × 1-in. jelly-roll pan. Line bottom with waxed paper, allowing 1-in. overhang; grease and flour paper.

In the top of a double boiler over low heat, melt chocolate with coffee, stirring frequently until smooth. Set aside.

With an electric mixer, beat egg yolks with half the sugar until pale and thick, about 5 minutes. Slowly beat in chocolate just until blended.

In another large bowl with electric mixer, beat egg whites and cream of tartar until stiff peaks form. Gradually sprinkle sugar over whites in 2 batches and continue beating until whites are stiff and glossy; beat in vanilla.

Stir 1 spoonful of whites into chocolate mixture to lighten, then fold in remaining whites. Spoon into prepared pan, spreading evenly.

Bake 12 to 15 minutes, or until cake springs back when touched with fingertip.

Meanwhile, dust tea towel with cocoa powder. When cake is done, turn out onto towel immediately and remove paper. Starting at a narrow end, roll cake and towel together jelly-roll fashion. Cool completely.

With electric mixer, whip cream and liqueur until soft peaks form. Beat 1 spoonful of cream into chestnut purée to lighten, then fold in remaining cream.

Unroll roulade and trim edges. Spread chestnut cream mixture to within 1 in. of edge of cake. Using the towel to lift the cake, roll cake jelly-roll fashion.

Place roulade seam-side down on a serving plate. Decorate the roulade with bands of sifted confectioners' sugar and candied chestnuts.

CHOCOLATE ANGEL CAKE

12 SERVINGS

This cake contains absolutely no fat at all and can be eaten plain, drizzled with a raspberry purée, chocolate syrup or chocolate sauce. I top it with an angel light Chocolate Whipped Cream.

1 1/4 cups confectioners' sugar
1 cup cake flour or 1 cup less 2 tbsp. all-purpose flour
1/3 cup unsweetened cocoa powder
12 egg whites (about 1 1/2 cups)
1 1/2 tsp. cream of tartar
1 1/2 tsp. vanilla extract
1 cup superfine sugar

CHOCOLATE WHIPPED CREAM
1/2 cup semisweet chocolate chips
1 1/3 cups whipping cream
1 tbsp. superfine sugar

Preheat oven to 350°F.

Into a bowl sift together confectioners' sugar, flour and cocoa powder; set aside.

In another bowl with electric mixer, beat egg whites, cream of tartar and vanilla until stiff peaks form. Gradually sprinkle in superfine sugar, 2 tbsp. at a time, beating well after each addition, until whites are stiff and glossy. Sprinkle flour mixture over and gently fold in just until blended. Gently spoon into *ungreased* 10-in. angel cake or tube pan, spreading evenly.

Bake 35 to 40 minutes, or until cake springs back when lightly touched with fingertip. Immediately invert cake in pan onto a funnel or bottle to cool completely.

With knife or metal spatula, loosen cake from pan and place on plate.

Prepare whipped cream. In a saucepan over low heat, melt half the chocolate chips with 1/3 cup cream, stirring until smooth; set aside to cool.

With electric mixer, whip remaining cream with superfine sugar until soft peaks form. Fold 1 spoonful of whipped cream into chocolate mixture to lighten, then quickly fold chocolate mixture into remaining cream. Spread on top of cake in a swirling pattern. Sprinkle the remaining chocolate chips over the top of cake.

MARBLED CHOCOLATE-PEANUT BUTTER BUNDT CAKE

12–14 SERVINGS

This is a moist, buttery cake which combines chocolate and peanut butter, a classic combination.

4 squares (4 oz.) unsweetened chocolate, chopped
1 cup (2 sticks) butter, softened
1 cup smooth peanut butter
2 cups sugar
5 eggs
2 cups all-purpose flour
2 tsp. baking powder
½ tsp. salt
½ cup milk
⅓ cup peanut butter-flavor pieces

CHOCOLATE-PEANUT BUTTER GLAZE

2 tbsp. butter, cut up
1 tbsp. smooth peanut butter
3 tbsp. light corn syrup
2 tbsp. water
1 tsp. vanilla extract
6 squares (6 oz.) semisweet chocolate

Preheat oven to 350°F. Generously grease and flour a 12-cup Bundt pan or 10-in tube pan.

In the top of a double boiler over low heat, melt chocolate.

With electric mixer, beat butter, peanut butter and sugar until light and creamy, about 5 minutes, scraping side of bowl occasionally. Add eggs, 1 at a time, beating well after each addition.

In another bowl, stir together flour, baking powder and salt. Add to peanut-butter mixture alternately with milk.

Pour half the batter into another bowl. Stir melted chocolate into one half until well blended. Stir peanut butter-flavored chips into the other half of batter.

Using a large spoon, drop alternate spoonfuls of chocolate batter and peanut-butter batter into the bundt pan. Using a knife, pull through the batters to create a marbled effect; do not touch side or bottom of pan or over-mix.

Bake 50 to 60 minutes, until top of cake springs back when touched with fingertip. Cool cake in pan on wire rack 10 minutes. Unmold onto rack to cool.

Meanwhile, prepare glaze. In a saucepan, combine all the ingredients. Melt over low heat, stirring until smooth. Cool slightly. When slightly thickened, drizzle glaze over cake allowing it to run down side.

SWEET SUCCESS

To avoid sticking, grease bundt or fluted pans very generously, especially the ridges, as you cannot use a knife to loosen edge.

MARBLED CHOCOLATE-PEANUT BUTTER BUNDT CAKE ▶

CHOCOLATE-SOUR CREAM CAKE

12–15 SERVINGS

Make the frosting while the cake is cooling and pour over the cake while both are warm for a rich, moist result.

½ cup (1 stick) butter, softened
1 cup sugar
4 eggs
2 cups all-purpose flour
½ cup unsweetened cocoa powder
1 tbsp. baking powder
1 tsp. baking soda
1 cup sour cream
1 cup semisweet chocolate chips

CHOCOLATE-SOUR CREAM FROSTING

9 squares (9 oz.) semisweet chocolate, chopped
3 tbsp. butter
½ cup sour cream
1 tsp. vanilla extract
3½ cups confectioners' sugar, sifted

Preheat oven to 350°F. Grease and flour 13- × 9-in. baking dish or cake pan.

With electric mixer, beat butter and sugar until light and creamy, about 5 minutes, scraping side of bowl occasionally. Add eggs, 1 at a time, beating well after each addition.

In another bowl, sift together flour, cocoa powder, baking powder and baking soda. Add to egg mixture alternately with sour cream, beating just until blended; stir in chocolate chips. Pour into prepared dish or pan and spread evenly.

Bake 25 to 30 minutes, until cake tester inserted in center comes out clean. Cool on wire rack.

Meanwhile, prepare frosting. In a saucepan over low heat, melt chocolate and butter, stirring until smooth. Cool about 10 minutes. Stir in sour cream and vanilla.

With wooden spoon, gradually beat in confectioners' sugar until frosting is thick and smooth. Pour over warm cake and spread evenly. Cool frosted cake completely.

SWEET SUCCESS

If using Chocolate-Sour Cream Frosting to fill and frost a layer cake or cupcakes, allow frosting to cool completely until spreading consistency.

SAUCY CHOCOLATE CAKE

8 SERVINGS

During baking, the cake batter sets and a creamy, saucy layer settles on the bottom, creating its own sauce.

1 cup all-purpose flour
½ cup sugar
5 tbsp. unsweetened cocoa powder
2 tsp. baking powder
½ tsp. salt
¾ cup milk
2 tbsp. butter
1 tsp. vanilla extract

TOPPING

¾ cup packed light brown sugar
½ cup chopped pecans (optional)
1¾ cups boiling water
confectioners' sugar for dusting

Preheat oven to 350°F. Lightly butter 8- × 8- × 2-in. baking dish.

Combine flour, sugar, 3 tbsp. cocoa powder, baking powder and salt. Stir in milk, butter and vanilla just until blended. Spoon into dish and spread evenly.

In another bowl, combine brown sugar, chopped nuts and remaining 2 tbsp. cocoa; gradually stir in boiling water until sugar dissolves. Gently pour over batter in baking dish.

Bake 25 to 30 minutes, until top of cake springs back when touched with fingertip. Cool 30 to 40 minutes on wire rack. Dust with confectioners' sugar and serve warm or chilled.

SWEET SUCCESS

This is an easy cake to prepare and bake at the last minute or when unexpected guests drop in. Most of the ingredients are pantry staples.

CHOCOLATE-MINT CUPCAKES

18–20 SERVINGS

These cupcakes are a moist, dark chocolate cake with a refreshing hint of mint echoed in the Chocolate Mint Glaze. They make an ideal snack for adults and children.

2 cups cake flour
1 tsp. baking soda
¼ tsp. salt
½ cup unsweetened cocoa powder
⅔ cup (1 stick plus 2 tbsp.) butter, softened
1½ cups superfine sugar
3 eggs
2 tsp. mint extract
1 cup milk

CHOCOLATE-MINT GLAZE
3 squares (3 oz.) semisweet chocolate
¼ cup (½ stick) butter
1 tsp. mint extract

Preheat oven to 350°F. Line twenty 2½-in. muffin cups with paper liners.

Sift together flour, baking soda, salt and cocoa powder.

In a second large bowl with electric mixer, beat butter and sugar until light and creamy, about 5 minutes. Add eggs, 1 at a time, beating well after each addition, then beat in mint extract.

On low speed, beat in flour-cocoa mixture alternately with milk just until blended. Spoon into paper liners filling each cup about three-quarters full.

Bake 12 to 15 minutes, until cake tester inserted in center, comes out clean; do not overbake. Cool in pan on wire rack 5 minutes; remove cupcakes to wire rack to cool completely.

Meanwhile, prepare glaze. In a saucepan over low heat, melt chocolate and butter, stirring until smooth. Remove from heat and stir in mint extract. Cool until spreadable.

BITTERSWEET CHOCOLATE-PECAN TORTE

16–19 SERVINGS

This European-style torte does not contain any flour, but uses ground pecans instead. Walnuts, hazelnuts or almonds can be substituted. The "cake" is baked in a water-bath to keep it extra moist.

7 squares (7 oz.) bittersweet or semisweet chocolate, chopped
⅔ cup (1 stick plus 2 tbsp.) unsalted butter, cut into pieces
4 eggs
½ cup sugar
2 tsp. vanilla extract
1 cup ground pecans (about 3½ oz.)

CHOCOLATE-HONEY GLAZE

4 squares (4 oz.) bittersweet or semisweet chocolate, chopped
¼ cup (½ stick) unsalted butter, cut into pieces
2 tbsp. honey
24 pecan halves for garnish

Preheat oven to 350°F. Grease an 8- × 2-in. springform pan; line bottom with waxed paper and grease waxed paper. Wrap bottom of pan in foil.

In a saucepan over low heat, melt chocolate and butter, stirring until smooth. Remove from heat.

With electric mixer, beat eggs with sugar and vanilla just until frothy, 1 to 2 minutes. Stir in melted chocolate and ground nuts until well blended. Pour into pan and tap gently on work surface to break any large air bubbles.

Place pan into larger roasting pan and pour boiling water into roasting pan, about ¾-in. up the side of springform pan. Bake 25 to 30 minutes, until edge of cake is set, but center is still soft. Remove pan from water-bath and remove foil. Cool on wire rack completely.

Meanwhile, prepare pecan halves for garnish. Place pecan halves on cookie sheet and bake 10 to 12 minutes, until just brown, stirring occasionally.

Prepare glaze. In a saucepan over low heat, melt chocolate, butter and honey, stirring until smooth; remove from heat. Carefully dip toasted nuts halfway into glaze and place on waxed paper-lined cookie sheet until set. Glaze will have thickened slightly.

Remove side of pan and turn cake onto wire rack placed over cookie sheet to catch any drips. Remove pan bottom and paper so bottom of cake is now the top. Pour thickened glaze over cake, tilting rack slightly to spread glaze. If necessary, use metal spatula to smooth side. Arrange nuts around outside edge of torte and leave glaze to set. With metal spatula, carefully slide cake onto serving dish.

SWEET SUCCESS

Cake can be baked 2 to 3 days ahead, wrapped tightly and refrigerated or even frozen. Bring to room temperature before glazing.

WHITE CHOCOLATE AND COCONUT LAYER CAKE

12–16 SERVINGS

Layered and frosted with a white chocolate-mousse mixture, then covered with whipped cream and garnished with strips of fresh coconut, this is a delicate white chocolate cake. White crème de cacao could replace the rum.

4 oz. fine-quality white chocolate, chopped
½ cup whipping cream
½ cup milk
1 tbsp. light rum
½ cup (1 stick) unsalted butter, softened
¾ cup sugar
3 eggs
2 cups all-purpose flour
1 tsp. baking powder
pinch salt
2 cups shredded sweetened coconut

WHITE CHOCOLATE MOUSSE

15 oz. fine-quality white chocolate, chopped
4½ cups whipping cream
¼ cup light rum
fresh coconut strips for garnish

Preheat oven to 350°F. Grease and flour two 9-in. cake pans.

In top of a double boiler over low heat, melt chocolate with cream, stirring until smooth. Stir in milk and rum; set aside to cool.

With electric mixer, beat butter with sugar until pale and thick, about 5 minutes. Add eggs, 1 at a time, beating well after each addition. In another bowl, stir together flour, baking powder and salt. Alternately add flour mixture and melted white chocolate in batches, just until blended; stir in 1 cup coconut. Pour batter into pans and spread evenly.

Bake 20 to 25 minutes, until cake tester inserted in centers comes out clean. Cool on wire rack 10 minutes. Unmold cakes onto wire rack and cool completely.

Meanwhile, prepare mousse. In a saucepan over low heat, melt white chocolate and 1½ cups cream, stirring frequently until smooth. Stir in rum, then pour into bowl. Refrigerate 1 to 1½ hours, until completely cold and thickened.

Whip remaining cream until soft peaks form. Stir 1 spoonful of cream into mousse mixture to lighten, then fold in about 1 cup whipped cream.

With serrated knife, slice both cake layers in half horizontally, making 4 layers. Place 1 layer on plate and spread one-sixth of mousse on top. Sprinkle with one-third of remaining coconut. Place second layer on top and spread with sixth of mousse. Sprinkle with another third of coconut. Place third layer on top and spread with another sixth of mousse and remaining coconut. Cover with last cake layer and frost top and side with remaining mousse.

Spread the remaining whipped cream over top and side of cake and garnish with fresh coconut strips.

SWEET SUCCESS

If fresh coconut is unavailable, use shredded sweetened coconut for garnish: Spread 1 cup coconut on cookie sheet and bake at 350°F 10 to 12 minutes, stirring twice, until golden. Press into side and sprinkle on top of cake.

For fresh coconut strips, use a swivel-bladed vegetable peeler to make paper-thin strips from fresh coconut pieces. Leave brown skin on pieces to create a pretty edge.

EASY CHOCOLATE TRUFFLE CAKE

16–20 SERVINGS

This must be the most chocolaty, yet easiest, dessert to make. It should be made at least one day before glazing.

6 squares (6 oz.) semisweet chocolate, chopped
3 squares (3 oz.) unsweetened chocolate, chopped
1 cup (2 sticks) unsalted butter, cut into pieces
¾ cup sugar
½ cup whipping cream
1 tbsp. vanilla extract
6 eggs

CHOCOLATE GLAZE

6 squares (6 oz.) bittersweet or semisweet chocolate, chopped
¼ cup (½ stick) butter, cut into pieces
whipped cream for garnish
rose petals for garnish

Preheat oven to 350°F. Generously grease a 9- × 2-in. round or scalloped springform pan; line bottom with waxed paper and grease waxed paper. Wrap bottom of pan in foil.

In a saucepan over low heat, melt chocolate, butter and sugar with cream, stirring frequently until smooth; cool slightly. Stir in vanilla.

With electric mixer, beat eggs lightly, about 1 minute. Slowly beat chocolate into eggs until blended. Pour into pan and tap gently on work surface to break any large air bubbles.

Place pan into larger roasting pan and pour boiling water into roasting pan, about ¾ in. up the side of springform pan. Bake 25 to 30 minutes, until edge of cake is set, but center is still soft. Remove pan from water-bath and remove foil. Cool on wire rack completely; cake will sink in center and may be cracked.

Remove side of pan and turn cake onto wire rack placed over cookie sheet to catch any drips. Remove pan bottom and paper.

Prepare glaze. In a saucepan over low heat, melt chocolate and butter, stirring until smooth. Pour over cake, tilting rack slightly to spread glaze. If necessary, use metal spatula to smooth

With metal spatula, carefully slide cake onto serving dish. If you like, pipe whipped cream border around edge. Dip rose petals in lightly-beaten egg white and then in caster sugar. Allow to stand on greaseproof paper for about 2 hours. Place on top of cake and serve with softly whipped cream on the side.

EASY CHOCOLATE TRUFFLE CAKE ►

BLACKOUT CAKE

12–16 SERVINGS

3 cups all-purpose flour
1 tbsp. baking soda
½ tsp. salt
4 squares (4 oz.) unsweetened chocolate, chopped
¾ cup (1½ sticks) unsalted butter, softened
3 cups sugar
3 eggs
2 tsp. vanilla extract
¾ cup buttermilk
1½ cups strong coffee (boiled) *or*
1 tbsp. instant coffee granules dissolved in 1½ cups boiling water

CHOCOLATE GANACHE FROSTING

1⅓ cups heavy cream
16 squares (1 lb.) bittersweet or
semisweet chocolate, chopped
¼ cup (½ stick) butter, cut into pieces
2 tsp. vanilla extract
grated chocolate for garnish
confectioners' sugar for dusting

Preheat oven to 350°F. Grease and flour two 9-in. cake pans.

Stir together flour, baking soda and salt. In the top of a double boiler over low heat, melt chocolate; set aside.

In a second bowl with electric mixer, beat butter with sugar until light and creamy, about 5 minutes. Add eggs, 1 at a time, beating well after each addition. Beat in chocolate and vanilla.

Add flour mixture to the batter in 2 additions alternately with the buttermilk; beat just until blended. At low speed, slowly beat in boiling coffee until smooth, scraping bowl once; batter will be thin. Pour into prepared pans.

Bake 25 to 30 minutes, or until cake tester inserted in centers comes out with just a few crumbs attached. Cool in pans on wire rack 10 minutes. Unmold and cool completely.

Meanwhile, prepare frosting. In a medium saucepan, bring cream to a boil. Remove from heat and immediately stir in chocolate until melted and smooth. Beat in butter and vanilla. Cool; refrigerate 45 to 55 minutes or until frosting is soft but spreadable.

Place 1 cake layer on a plate and cover with one-third of the frosting. Place second layer on top and frost top and side with remaining frosting. Press grated chocolate onto side of cake and sprinkle on top. Dust top with confectioners' sugar.

CHOCOLATE-RASPBERRY TORTE

10 SERVINGS

A most elegant, delicious torte, ideal for any special occasion. The flavor of chocolate and raspberry is one of my favorites. This can be made without the fresh raspberries, but they add a special touch.

4 squares (4 oz.) semisweet or bittersweet chocolate, chopped
1 cup ground blanched almonds
¼ cup all-purpose flour
½ cup (1 stick) butter, softened
½ cup sugar
4 eggs, separated
¼ tsp. cream of tartar

CHOCOLATE-RASPBERRY GANACHE FROSTING AND FILLING
1 cup heavy cream
1 cup seedless raspberry preserves
10 squares (10 oz.) bittersweet or semisweet chocolate, chopped
2 tbsp. butter, cut into pieces
4 tbsp. raspberry-flavor liqueur
½ pt. fresh raspberries, 8 or 10 reserved for garnish
chocolate leaves (see Decorating with Chocolate) for garnish

Preheat oven to 350°F. Grease bottom and side of 15½- × 10½- × 1-in. jelly-roll pan. Line bottom with waxed paper, allowing 1-in. overhang; grease and flour paper.

In the top of a double boiler over low heat, melt chocolate, stirring frequently until smooth. Set aside to cool.

In a bowl, mix ground almonds and flour until blended. In another bowl with electric mixer, beat butter and ¼ cup sugar until pale and creamy, about 3 minutes. Add the egg yolks, 1 at a time, beating well after each addition. Slowly beat in melted chocolate until well blended, scraping bowl occasionally.

In a large bowl with electric mixer, beat egg whites with the cream of tartar until stiff peaks form. Gradually sprinkle remaining ¼ cup sugar over whites in 2 batches, beating until whites are stiff and glossy.

Stir 1 spoonful of whites into chocolate mixture to lighten, then fold in remaining whites and almond-flour mixture alternately just until blended. Spoon into pan, spreading evenly.

Bake 10 to 12 minutes, or until cake springs back when touched with fingertip.

Cool cake in pan on wire rack 10 minutes. Using paper corners as a guide, lift cake out of pan onto rack to cool completely.

Meanwhile, prepare frosting. In a saucepan, bring cream and ½ cup raspberry preserves to a boil. Remove from heat and immediately stir in chocolate until melted and smooth. Beat in butter and half the raspberry-flavor liqueur. Cool frosting mixture, then refrigerate until it reaches a spreading consistency, about 1 hour; stir occasionally.

Turn cake onto work surface, bottom side up. Trim cake edges and cut cake crosswise into 3 equal strips. In a saucepan, melt remaining preserves and raspberry-flavor liqueur, stirring until smooth; spoon equally over each cake strip and leave to soak in, 2 to 3 minutes.

Place 1 cake strip on wire rack over a cookie sheet to catch drips. Spread with about 1 cup chilled frosting. Sprinkle with half the raspberries. Top with second cake strip and spread with 1 cup frosting and remaining raspberries. Place third cake strip on top, top-side up. With metal spatula, spread remaining frosting over top and sides of torte. Leave to set.

With metal spatula, slide cake onto serving dish. Garnish top of torte with chocolate leaves and raspberries.

VARIATION

For a lighter look, beat the frosting for 30–45 seconds until light and fluffy. Decorate and frost the torte immediately before the frosting hardens.

BLACK FOREST CAKE

10 SERVINGS

A classic European-style cake based on a cocoa sponge cake. The combination of chocolate, cherries and cream is a delicious one. Try poaching your own fresh cherries in a sugar syrup when they are in season.

⅔ cup cake flour
⅓ cup unsweetened cocoa powder
½ tsp. baking powder
5 eggs, separated
¾ cup plus 2 tbsp. sugar
¼ tsp. cream of tartar
5 tbsp. butter, melted and cooled

CHERRY FILLING

1 15-oz. can sour or black cherries in juice or syrup, pitted
5 tbsp. cherry-flavor liqueur
2 tbsp. cornstarch, dissolved in 2 tbsp. water
2 cups whipping cream
2 tbsp. superfine sugar
Easy Chocolate Curls (see Decorating with Chocolate) for garnish
candied or maraschino cherries for garnish

Preheat oven to 350°F. Grease bottom and side of 8-in. springform pan. Line bottom with waxed paper; grease paper and flour pan.

Sift together flour, cocoa powder and baking powder; set aside. In a bowl with electric mixer, beat egg yolks with ¾ cup sugar until pale and thick, about 5 minutes.

In another bowl with electric mixer, beat egg whites and cream of tartar until stiff peaks form. Sprinkle in remaining 2 tbsp. sugar and beat until stiff and glossy.

Stir 1 spoonful of whites into yolk mixture to lighten. Fold in flour-cocoa mixture and remaining egg whites alternately just until blended. Pour melted butter over and fold in just until blended. Spoon into pan spreading evenly.

Bake 30 to 35 minutes, until cake tester inserted in center comes out clean. Cool in pan on wire rack 10 minutes. Remove side and bottom of pan and cool completely. Peel off paper.

Meanwhile, prepare filling. Drain cherries, reserving juice. Mix 3 tbsp. cherry juice with 3 tbsp. cherry-flavor liqueur; set aside. In a saucepan, stir together remaining cherry juice and cornstarch mixture. Bring to a boil, then simmer 2 to 3 minutes, until thickened. Stir in cherries and set aside to cool.

Whip cream, sugar and remaining cherry-flavor liqueur until soft peaks form. Reserve about ½ cup cream for garnish.

With a serrated knife, cut cake horizontally into 3 layers. Place bottom layer on a plate. Sprinkle over one-third cherry-juice syrup and spread with about ¾ cup whipped cream. Spoon half the cherry mixture evenly over cream and cover with second cake layer. Sprinkle third of the cherry-juice syrup over and another ¾ cup whipped cream. Spoon remaining cherry mixture over. Sprinkle cut-side of third cake layer with remaining cherry-juice syrup and place cut-side down over cherry layer. Frost top and side of cake with remaining whipped cream.

Press chocolate curls onto side of cake. Spoon reserved cream into small pastry bag fitted with a medium star tip and pipe 10 rosettes evenly around cake. Top each with a candied or maraschino cherry. Refrigerate.

SWEET SUCCESS

Garnish cake with cherries at the last minute to avoid any color from cherries bleeding into cream.

CHOCOLATE-BANANA SWIRL CHEESECAKE

16 SERVINGS

I first made this cheesecake in an effort to use some overripe bananas in the kitchen. It uses the flavors of a banana split with hot fudge sauce. The banana mixture is highly perfumed and contrasts with the soft, fudgy chocolate swirls.

CRUMB CRUST

5 oz. ginger snaps (16–18)
½ cup walnuts
¼ cup (½ stick) butter, melted
½ tsp. ground ginger

FILLING

4 squares (4 oz.) semisweet or bittersweet chocolate, chopped
¼ cup (½ stick) butter, cut into pieces
5 8-oz. packages cream cheese, softened
1¼ cups sugar
1 tbsp. vanilla extract
5 eggs
1 cup sour cream
about 3 ripe bananas
1 tbsp. lemon juice

Preheat oven to 350°F. Lightly grease a 10- × 3-in. springform pan.

In a food processor, process ginger snaps and walnuts until fine crumbs form. Pour in melted butter and ginger. Process just until blended. Pat onto bottom and to within ½ in. of top of side of pan.

Bake 5 to 7 minutes, just until set. Remove to wire rack to cool while preparing filling. Lower oven temperature to 300°F.

In a saucepan over low heat, melt chocolate and butter, stirring frequently until smooth. Set aside to cool.

With electric mixer, beat cream cheese and sugar until smooth, 2 to 4 minutes; stir in vanilla. Add eggs, 1 at a time, beating well after each addition, scraping bowl occasionally, then blend in sour cream. Pour about 1½ cups of cream-cheese mixture into a bowl and stir in melted chocolate until well blended. Set mixture aside.

In a second bowl, mash bananas with lemon juice to make 1½ cups, then beat into remaining cream-cheese mixture until well blended. Pour banana mixture into baked crust. Drop spoonfuls of chocolate mixture over banana mixture in a circle about 1 in. from side of pan. With a spoon or knife, swirl chocolate mixture into banana mixture creating a marbled effect. Do not overmix. Place pan on cookie sheet; place small pan of water on floor of oven to create moisture during baking.

Bake 50 to 60 minutes, until edge of cheesecake is set, but center is still soft. Turn off oven and leave to stand 30 minutes; this helps prevent cracking. Remove to wire rack, run knife around edge of cheesecake in pan to separate it from side; this also helps prevent cracking. Cool completely, then refrigerate, loosely covered, overnight.

To serve, run knife around edge of pan to loosen cheesecake. Remove side of pan. If you like, slide knife under crust to separate cheesecake from bottom, then, with metal spatula, slide onto serving plate. Alternatively, leave cheesecake on pan bottom to avoid breaking crust or surface and serve from pan bottom.

WHITE CHOCOLATE CHEESECAKE

16–20 SERVINGS

White chocolate seems the perfect marriage with a cream-cheese filling. This rich, creamy cake is based on my classic New York-style cheesecake, but has a more elegant European look!

CRUMB CRUST

5 oz. graham crackers (16–18)
⅓ cup pecan or walnut halves
¼ cup (½ stick) butter, melted
½ teaspoon ground cinnamon

FILLING

12 oz. fine-quality white chocolate, chopped
½ cup whipping cream
3 8-oz. packages cream cheese
⅓ cup sugar
4 eggs
1 tbsp. vanilla extract
cocoa powder for dusting (optional)
White and Dark Chocolate Curls (see Decorating with Chocolate) for garnish

SOUR CREAM TOPPING

1¾ cups sour cream
¼ cup sugar
1 tsp. vanilla extract

Preheat oven to 350°F. Lightly grease a 9- × 3-in. springform pan.

Prepare crust. In a food processor, process graham crackers and pecans until fine crumbs form. Pour in melted butter and cinnamon. Process just until blended. Pat onto bottom and to within ½ in. of top of side of pan.

Bake 5 to 7 minutes, just until set. Remove to wire rack to cool while preparing filling. Lower oven temperature to 300°F.

In a saucepan over low heat, melt chocolate with cream, stirring frequently until smooth. Set aside to cool.

With electric mixer, beat cream cheese and sugar until smooth, 2 to 4 minutes. Add eggs, 1 at a time, beating well after each addition, scraping bowl occasionally. Slowly beat in white-chocolate mixture and vanilla just until blended. Pour into baked crust. Place on cookie sheet; place small pan of water on floor of oven to create moisture during baking.

Bake 45 to 55 minutes, or until edge of cheesecake is firm but center is still slightly soft. Remove cheesecake to wire rack while preparing topping. Increase oven temperature to 400°F.

In a bowl, beat sour cream, sugar and vanilla. Pour over cheesecake and return to oven. Bake 5 minutes longer. Remove to wire rack to cool to room temperature. Run knife around edge of cake in pan to separate it from side; this helps prevent cracking. Cool completely, then refrigerate overnight.

To serve, run knife around edge of pan to loosen cheesecake. Remove side of pan. If you like, slide knife under crust to separate cheesecake from bottom, then, with metal spatula, slide onto serving plate. Alternatively, leave cheesecake on pan bottom to avoid breaking crust or surface and serve from pan bottom.

Dust top of cheesecake with cocoa or garnish with white and dark chocolate curls.

SWEET SUCCESS

Use back of spoon to press crumbs to bottom and side of pan.

TRIPLE CHOCOLATE CHEESECAKE

16–20 SERVINGS

This is a very rich, deep-chocolate cheesecake surrounded by a chocolate crust, then topped with a chocolate glaze and cocoa finish.

8 oz. chocolate wafers (24–26)
¼ cup (½ stick) butter, melted
½ tsp. ground cinnamon

FILLING

16 squares (1 lb.) semisweet or bittersweet chocolate, chopped
½ cup (1 stick) butter, cut into pieces
1 cup sour cream
4 8-oz. packages cream cheese, softened
1 cup sugar
5 eggs
1 tbsp. vanilla extract

CHOCOLATE GLAZE

4 squares (4 oz.) bittersweet or semisweet chocolate, chopped
½ cup heavy cream
1 tsp. vanilla extract
cocoa

Preheat oven to 350°F. Lightly grease bottom and side of 10- × 3-in. springform pan.

Prepare crust. In a food processor, process chocolate wafers until fine crumbs form. Pour in melted butter and cinnamon. Process just until blended. Pat onto bottom and to within ½ in. of top of side of pan.

Bake 5 to 7 minutes, just until set. Remove to wire rack to cool while preparing filling. Lower oven temperature to 325°F.

In a saucepan over low heat, melt chocolate and butter, stirring frequently until smooth. Set aside to cool; stir in sour cream.

With electric mixer, beat cream cheese and sugar until smooth, 2 to 4 minutes. Add eggs, 1 at a time, beating well after each addition, scraping bowl occasionally. Slowly beat in chocolate mixture and vanilla just until blended. Pour into baked crust. Place pan on cookie sheet; place small pan of water on floor of oven to create moisture.

Bake 1 to 1½ hours, or until edge of cheesecake is set but center is still slightly soft. Turn off the oven but leave cheesecake in the oven for another 30 minutes. Remove to wire rack to cool. Run knife around edge of cheesecake in pan to separate it from side; this helps prevent cracking. Cool to room temperature.

Prepare glaze. In a saucepan, melt chocolate with cream and vanilla, stirring until smooth. Cool and leave to thicken slightly, 10 to 15 minutes. Pour over warm cake in pan; cool glazed cake completely. Using strips of waxed paper dust cocoa on in horizontal bands across the top of the cake. Refrigerate, loosely covered, overnight.

To serve, run knife around edge of pan to loosen cheesecake. Remove side of pan. If you like, slide knife under crust to separate cheesecake from bottom, and, with metal spatula, slide onto serving plate. Alternatively, leave cheesecake on pan bottom to avoid breaking crust or surface and serve from pan bottom.

Pies and Pastries

ANTOINE'S CHOCOLATE AND PINE NUT TART

7–8 SERVINGS

My friend Antoine Bouterin, the chef at Le Perigord in New York City, taught me how to make this tart when we toured the U.S. giving cooking demonstrations. I never forgot the combination of warm chocolate, toasted pine nuts and orange zest in a creamy custard—simple, but sometimes the simplest things are best. This is my variation.

SWEET FRENCH TART PASTRY

1½ cups all-purpose flour
¼ cup superfine sugar
¼ teaspoon salt
½ cup (1 stick) butter, cut into small pieces
3 egg yolks, lightly beaten
1-2 tbsp. iced water

FILLING

2 eggs
⅓ cup sugar
grated zest of 1 orange
1 tbsp. orange-flavor liqueur
1 cup whipping cream
4 squares (4 oz.) bittersweet or semisweet chocolate, chopped
⅓ cup pine nuts, toasted (2½ oz.)

GLAZE

1 orange
½ cup water
¼ cup sugar

Prepare pastry. In a food processor fitted with metal blade, process flour, sugar and salt to blend. Add butter and process 15 to 20 seconds, until mixture resembles coarse crumbs. Add egg yolks and using *pulse action*, process just until dough begins to stick together; *do not allow dough to form a ball* or pastry will be tough. If dough appears dry, add 1-2 tbsp. iced water, little by little, just until dough holds together.

Turn dough onto lightly floured work surface and using a pastry scraper to scrape dough, knead gently until well blended. Shape dough into flat disk and wrap tightly in plastic wrap. Refrigerate 4 to 5 hours.

Lightly butter a 9-in. tart pan with removable bottom. Soften dough 5 to 10 minutes at room temperature. On a well-floured surface, roll out dough into an 11-in. circle about ¼-in. thick. Roll dough loosely around rolling pin and unroll over tart pan; ease dough into pan.

With floured fingers, press overhang down slightly toward center, making top edge thicker, then roll rolling pin over pan edge to cut off excess dough. Press thicker top edge against side of pan to form rim about ¼-in. higher than pan. Using thumb and forefinger, crimp edge. Prick bottom of dough with fork. Refrigerate 1 hour.

Preheat oven to 400°F. Line tart shell with foil or parchment paper and fill with dry beans or rice. Bake 5 minutes, lift out foil with beans and bake 5 minutes longer, just until set. Remove to wire rack to cool slightly. Lower oven temperature to 375°F.

In a bowl, beat together eggs, sugar, orange zest and orange-flavor liqueur. Blend in the cream.

Sprinkle chopped chocolate evenly over bottom of tart shell, then sprinkle pine nuts over. Place pan on cookie sheet and gently pour egg-and-cream mixture into shell.

Bake 30 to 35 minutes, until pastry is golden and egg mixture is set. Remove to wire rack to cool 10 minutes.

Prepare garnish. With swivel-bladed vegetable peeler, remove thin strips of orange zest and cut into julienne strips. In a saucepan over high heat, bring strips, water and sugar to a boil. Boil 5 to 8 minutes, until syrup is thickened; stir in 1 tbsp. cold water.

With a pastry brush, glaze tart with sugar syrup and arrange julienne orange strips over top. Remove side of pan and slide tart onto plate. Serve tart warm.

CHOCOLATE-PECAN PIE

8–10 SERVINGS

It hardly seems possible to improve on classic pecan pie, that is, of course, unless you add chocolate. The pastry is almost unsweetened to balance the rich filling. Serve with softly whipped cream.

1¼ cups all-purpose flour
1 tbsp. superfine sugar
½ tsp. salt
½ cup (1 stick) butter, cut into small pieces
½ cup iced water

FILLING

3 squares (3 oz.) unsweetened chocolate, chopped
2 tbsp. butter, cut into pieces
3 eggs
¾ cup packed light brown sugar
¾ cup light corn syrup
1 tbsp. vanilla extract
2 cups pecan halves
½ cup (3 oz.) milk or semisweet chocolate chips (optional)

Prepare piecrust. In a food processor fitted with metal blade, process flour, sugar and salt to blend. Add butter and process 15 to 20 seconds, until mixture resembles coarse crumbs. With machine running, add iced water through feed tube, just until dough begins to stick together; *do not allow dough to form a ball* or pastry will be tough.

Turn dough onto floured work surface, shape into flat disk and wrap tightly in plastic wrap. Refrigerate 1 hour.

Lightly butter a 9-in. pie plate. Soften dough 10 to 15 minutes at room temperature. On a well-floured surface, roll out dough into a 12-in. circle about ¼-in. thick. Roll dough loosely around rolling pin and unroll over pie plate; ease dough into plate.

With kitchen scissors, trim dough, leaving about a ¼-in. overhang; flatten to rim of pie plate pressing slightly toward center of plate. With small knife, cut out hearts or other shapes from dough trimmings. Brush dough edge with water and press dough shapes to edge. Prick bottom of dough with fork. Refrigerate 30 minutes.

Preheat oven to 400°F. Line pie shell with foil or parchment paper and fill with dry beans or rice. Bake 5 minutes, then lift out foil with beans and bake 5 minutes longer. Remove to wire rack to cool slightly. Lower oven temperature to 375°F.

In a saucepan over low heat, melt chocolate and butter, stirring until smooth. Set aside.

In a bowl, beat together eggs, sugar, corn syrup and vanilla. Slowly beat in melted chocolate. Sprinkle pecan halves and chocolate chips (if using) over bottom of pastry. Place pie plate on cookie sheet and carefully pour in chocolate mixture.

Bake 35 to 40 minutes, until chocolate mixture is set, top may crack slightly. If pastry edges begin to overbrown, cover with strips of foil. Remove to wire rack to cool. Serve warm with softly whipped cream.

VARIATION

For an extra rich treat use the chocolate pastry described on page 39.

CHOCOLATE CREAM PIE

8 SERVINGS

A *classic, old-fashioned dessert; under a cloud of whipped cream is a deep, chocolate custard enclosed in a chocolate crumb crust. The whipped cream topping is lightened by adding beaten egg whites.*

8 oz. chocolate wafers (24–26)
¼ cup (½ stick) butter, melted
4 squares (4 oz.) bittersweet or semisweet chocolate, chopped
2 squares (2 oz.) unsweetened chocolate, chopped
1 cup whipping cream
⅓ cup cornstarch
1 tbsp. all-purpose flour
½ cup superfine sugar
2¾ cups milk
5 egg yolks
3 tbsp. butter, softened

LIGHT WHIPPED CREAM
1½ cups heavy cream
2 egg whites
¼ tsp. cream of tartar
¼ cup superfine sugar
2 tsp. vanilla extract
unsweetened cocoa powder for dusting

Preheat oven to 350°F. Lightly butter a 9-in. pie plate.

In a food processor, process chocolate wafers until fine crumbs form. Pour in melted butter and process just until blended. Pat onto bottom and side of pie plate.

Bake for 5 to 7 minutes, just until set. Remove to wire rack to cool completely.

In a saucepan over low heat, melt chocolate with 1 cup whipping cream, stirring until smooth. Set aside.

In another saucepan, combine cornstarch, flour and sugar. Gradually stir in milk and cook over medium heat until thickened and bubbling.

In a bowl, beat egg yolks lightly. Slowly pour over 1 cup hot milk into yolks, stirring constantly. Return egg-yolk mixture to pan and bring to a gentle boil, stirring constantly. Cook 1 minute longer. Stir in the butter and melted chocolate until well blended. Pour into prepared crust and place a piece of plastic wrap directly against surface of filling to prevent a skin forming. Cool, then refrigerate until completely chilled.

With electric mixer, whip cream until soft peaks form. In another bowl with electric mixer and clean blades, beat egg whites and cream of tartar until stiff peaks form. Gradually sprinkle sugar over in 2 batches, beating well after each addition, until whites are stiff and glossy. Beat in vanilla.

Fold 1 spoonful of whites into cream to lighten, then fold remaining whites into cream. Peel plastic wrap from chilled custard; spread cream onto custard in a swirling pattern. Dust cream lightly with cocoa powder.

WHITE CHOCOLATE AND BANANA CREAM TART

8 SERVINGS

A luscious combination of a white-chocolate-flavored custard, bananas and whipped cream enclosed in a crisp pastry case with a little coconut for extra texture.

1½ cups all-purpose flour
1 cup shredded sweetened coconut
½ cup (1 stick) butter, softened
2 tbsp. superfine sugar
2 egg yolks
½ tsp. almond extract

WHITE CHOCOLATE CUSTARD

5 oz. fine-quality white chocolate, chopped
½ cup heavy cream
⅓ cup cornstarch
1 tbsp. all-purpose flour
⅓ cup sugar
2 cups milk
5 egg yolks
2½ cups whipping cream
½ tsp. almond extract
3 very ripe bananas
⅔ cup chopped almonds, toasted

Prepare pastry. With electric mixer at low speed, combine flour, coconut, butter, sugar, egg yolks and almond extract until well blended.

With fingers or back of a spoon, press dough onto bottom and side of a lightly-buttered, deep 9-in. tart pan with removable bottom. Prick dough with fork. Refrigerate 30 minutes.

Preheat oven to 350°F. Line tart shell with foil or parchment paper; fill with dry beans or rice. Bake 10 minutes. Carefully lift out foil with beans and bake 5 to 7 minutes longer, until golden. Remove to wire rack to cool completely.

Prepare custard. In a saucepan over low heat, melt white chocolate with cream, stirring until smooth. Set aside.

In another saucepan, combine cornstarch, flour and sugar. Gradually stir in the milk and cook over medium heat until thickened and bubbling.

Beat egg yolks lightly. Slowly pour about 1 cup hot milk into the yolks, stirring constantly. Return egg-yolk mixture to the pan and bring to a gentle boil, stirring constantly. Cook 1 to 2 minutes longer. Stir in the melted chocolate until well blended. Cool to room temperature, stirring frequently to prevent a skin from forming.

With electric mixer, beat the whipping cream with the almond extract until soft peaks form. Fold about ½ cup whipped cream into white chocolate custard.

Slice bananas and line bottom of pastry shell with the slices. Pour the white-chocolate custard over and spread evenly. Remove side of pan and slide onto plate.

Spoon remaining cream into large pastry bag fitted with a medium star tip. Pipe cream in scroll pattern in parallel rows, ½-in. apart. Sprinkle chopped toasted almonds between rows.

SWEET SUCCESS

To prevent a skin forming on the custard, do not stir, but dot the top with tiny cubes of butter. The butter melts over the hot surface of the cream and prevents a skin from forming. When ready to use, simply stir the butter into the cream.

MOCHA-FUDGE PIE WITH ESPRESSO CUSTARD CREAM

10 SERVINGS

Even the most serious of chocolate lovers will be satisfied with this crustless, fudgy dessert. It is crisp on the outside but soft and brownie-like near the center. The coffee custard cream is a welcome contrast to the rich, dense chocolate.

4 squares (4 oz.) unsweetened chocolate, chopped
½ cup (1 stick) butter, cut into pieces
4 eggs
1 tbsp. light corn syrup
1⅓ cups sugar
1 tbsp. instant espresso powder, dissolved in 1–2 tbsp. hot water
1 tsp. ground cinnamon
3 tbsp. milk

ESPRESSO CUSTARD CREAM

3 cups milk
1 tbsp. instant espresso powder, dissolved in 1–2 tbsp. hot water
¾ cup sugar
6 egg yolks
2 tsp. cornstarch
2 tbsp. coffee-flavor liqueur
whipped cream and chocolate coffee beans for garnish (optional)

Preheat oven to 350°F. Lightly grease a 9-in. deep pie plate.

In a saucepan over low heat, melt chocolate and butter, stirring until smooth. Set aside.

In a bowl, beat eggs lightly. Blend in corn syrup, sugar, dissolved espresso powder, cinnamon and milk. Stir in chocolate mixture until well blended. Place pie plate on a cookie sheet. Pour chocolate mixture into pie plate.

Bake 20 to 25 minutes, or until the edge is set but center is still almost liquid. Remove to wire rack to cool completely; top may crack slightly.

Prepare custard. In a saucepan over medium heat, bring milk and dissolved espresso powder to a boil. In a bowl, beat sugar and egg yolks until pale and thick, 3 to 5 minutes. Stir in cornstarch just until blended.

Slowly pour about 1 cup hot milk into yolks, stirring constantly. Return yolk mixture to pan and cook over low heat, stirring constantly, until the sauce thickens, 5 to 8 minutes; *do not allow sauce to boil or it will curdle.* Strain into a *chilled* bowl and stir until slightly cool. Stir in coffee-flavor liqueur and cool completely. Refrigerate until ready to serve.

To serve, place a spoonful of custard on a dessert plate and place a slice of tart on the pool of sauce. If you like, garnish with softly whipped cream and chocolate coffee beans.

SWEET SUCCESS

To help custard sauces to cool quickly and stop cooking instantly, strain the thickened custard into a metal bowl placed over another bowl of water with ice cubes; stir frequently until custard is just body temperature. This stops further cooking and prevents a skin from forming.

CHOCOLATE TRUFFLE TART

10 SERVINGS

A pure chocolate truffle mixture is contained in a chocolate pastry in this delicious tart. The chocolate-on-chocolate drizzling is more for effect than flavor but the tart is equally delicious without it.

1 cup all-purpose flour
⅓ cup unsweetened cocoa powder
¼ cup superfine sugar
½ tsp. salt
½ cup (1 stick) well-chilled butter, cut into pieces
1 egg yolk
1–2 tbsp. iced water

TRUFFLE FILLING
1⅓ cups heavy cream
12 squares (12 oz.) bittersweet chocolate, chopped
3 tbsp. butter, cut into pieces
1–2 tbsp. orange-flavor liqueur or brandy (optional)
1 oz. fine-quality white chocolate, melted

Prepare pastry. Into a bowl, sift flour and cocoa powder. In a food processor fitted with metal blade, process flour mixture, sugar and salt to blend. Add butter and process 15 to 20 seconds, until mixture resembles coarse crumbs.

In another bowl, lightly beat egg yolk with 2 tbsp. iced water. Add to flour mixture and using *pulse action* process just until dough begins to stick together; *do not allow dough to form into a ball* or pastry will be tough. Dough should be soft and creamy and may be difficult to handle. Place a piece of plastic wrap on work surface. Turn out dough onto plastic wrap. Use plastic wrap to help shape dough into flat disk and wrap tightly. Refrigerate 1 to 2 hours.

Lightly grease a 9-in. tart pan with removable bottom. Soften dough 5 to 10 minutes at room temperature. Roll out dough between 2 sheets of waxed paper or plastic wrap to an 11-in. circle about ¼ in. thick. Peel off top sheet of waxed paper or plastic wrap and invert dough into pan. Remove bottom layer of paper or wrap. Press dough onto bottom and side of pan. Prick bottom of dough with fork. Refrigerate 1 hour.

Preheat oven to 375°F. Line tart shell with foil or parchment paper; fill with dried beans or rice. Bake 5 to 7 minutes; lift out foil with beans and bake 5 to 7 minutes longer, just until set; pastry may look slightly underdone on bottom, but it will dry out. Remove to wire rack to cool completely.

In a saucepan over medium heat, bring cream to a boil. Remove pan from heat and stir in chocolate until melted and smooth. Stir in butter and liqueur.

Strain into tart shell; tilting slightly to even surface, but do not touch surface.

Spoon melted white chocolate into paper cone (see Decorating with Chocolate) and cut tip about ¼ in. in diameter. Drizzle white chocolate over surface of dark chocolate in an abstract design.

Refrigerate 2 to 3 hours, until set. To serve, leave tart to soften slightly at room temperature, about 30 minutes.

SWEET SUCCESS

This tart can be made 2 days ahead and stored, covered, in the refrigerator. To store tarts or desserts without destroying the top or the garnish, place on a cookie sheet and cover with a large overturned bowl.

WHITE CHOCOLATE MOUSSE AND STRAWBERRY TART

10–12 SERVINGS

This is a luscious combination of white chocolate mousse and ripe, fragrant strawberries in a butter-rich crust. It can be made with other soft fruits such as raspberries or blackberries.

½ cup (1 stick) butter, softened
¼ cup superfine sugar
½ tsp. salt
3 egg yolks
1 tsp. vanilla extract
1¼ cups all-purpose flour

WHITE CHOCOLATE MOUSSE FILLING
9 oz. white chocolate, chopped
3 tbsp. cherry-flavor liqueur
2 tbsp. water
1½ cups heavy cream
2 egg whites (optional)
¼ tsp. cream of tartar (optional)

STRAWBERRY FILLING
2 lbs. fresh, ripe strawberries
2 tbsp. cherry-flavor liqueur
1 oz. white chocolate, melted, *or* White Chocolate Curls (see Decorating with Chocolate) *or* 2 tbsp. seedless strawberry preserves, melted and cooled, for garnish

Prepare pastry. In a bowl with a hand-held electric mixer, beat butter with sugar and salt until creamy, about 2 minutes. Add egg yolks and vanilla and beat until smooth. Add half the flour to the butter-egg mixture, then stir in remaining flour by hand until well blended.

Place a piece of plastic wrap on work surface. Scrape dough onto plastic wrap. Use plastic wrap to help shape dough into flat disk and wrap tightly. Refrigerate 1 hour.

Lightly butter a 10-in. tart pan with removable bottom. Soften dough 10 minutes at room temperature. On a well-floured surface, roll out dough to 11½- to 12-in. circle about ⅛-in. thick. Roll dough loosely around rolling pin and unroll over tart pan. Ease dough into pan, patching if necessary.

With floured fingers, press overhang down slightly toward center, making top edge thicker. Roll rolling pin over pan edge to cut off excess dough. Press thicker top edge against side of pan to form rim about ¼-in. higher than pan. Using thumb and forefinger, crimp edge. Prick bottom of dough with fork. Refrigerate 1 hour.

Preheat oven to 375°F. Line tart shell with foil or parchment paper; fill with dry beans or rice. Bake 10 minutes; lift out foil with beans and bake 5 to 7 minutes longer until set and golden. Remove to wire rack to cool completely.

Cut strawberries in half lengthwise. In a bowl, mash about 1 cup strawberry halves with 2 tbsp. cherry-flavor liqueur. Set remaining berries and mashed berries aside.

Prepare mousse. In a saucepan over low heat, melt white chocolate with 3 tbsp. cherry-flavor liqueur, water and ¼ cup cream, stirring until smooth. Set aside to cool.

With electric mixer, beat remaining cream until soft peaks form. Stir 1 spoonful of cream into the chocolate mixture to lighten, then fold in remaining cream. If you like, beat egg whites with the cream of tartar until stiff peaks form then fold them into the chocolate cream mixture to make a lighter, softer mousse.

Pour about one-third of the mousse mixture into the cooled tart shell. Spread mashed berries evenly over the mousse, then cover with the remaining mousse mixture.

To serve, arrange sliced strawberries cut side up in concentric circles around tart to cover mousse. Remove side of pan and slide tart onto serving plate. Spoon melted white chocolate into a paper cone (see Decorating with Chocolate) and drizzle white chocolate over tart; alternatively, garnish center with white chocolate curls, or glaze with seedless strawberry preserves.

SWEET SUCCESS

Be sure to allow the melted white chocolate to cool to below body temperature so it does not deflate the whipped cream. A small dab should feel cool when touched to your upper lip, about 85°F.

The tart shell can be made ahead, but the shell should be filled and assembled the same day to be served to prevent the berries from bleeding into the mousse mixture and the mousse from becoming too firm when refrigerated.

CHOCOLATE-CHOCOLATE CREAM PUFFS

ABOUT 12 LARGE PUFFS

With chocolate choux pastry and filled with a rich chocolate pastry cream, these cream puffs are then covered with a creamy chocolate topping. They can be made any size from mini to maxi!

1 cup all-purpose flour
2 tbsp. unsweetened cocoa powder
1 cup water
½ tsp. salt
1 tbsp. sugar
½ cup (1 stick) butter, cut into pieces
5 eggs

CHOCOLATE PASTRY CREAM

5 squares (5 oz.) semisweet chocolate, chopped
2 cups milk
6 egg yolks
½ cup sugar
5 tbsp. all-purpose flour
½ cup whipping cream, whipped to soft peaks

CHOCOLATE SAUCE

¼ cup (½ stick) butter, cut into pieces
8 squares (8 oz.) bittersweet or semisweet chocolate, chopped
1¼ cups whipping cream

Preheat oven to 425°F. Lightly grease 2 large cookie sheets.

Sift together flour and cocoa powder. In a saucepan over medium heat, bring water, salt, sugar and butter to a boil; the butter should just be melted when the water boils. Remove from heat and add flour mixture all at once, stirring vigorously until well blended and dough pulls away from side of pan. Return to the heat to cook 1 minute, stirring constantly. Remove from heat.

With an electric mixer or by hand, beat in eggs, 1 at a time, beating well after each addition; dough should be thick and shiny and just fall from a spoon.

Spoon dough into a large pastry bag fitted with a star or plain tip. Pipe 12 mounds about 3 in. across, at least 2 in. apart onto cookie sheets.

Bake 35 to 40 minutes, until puffed and firm. Turn off oven. Using a serrated knife, slice off top third of puff; return opened puffs, cut-sides up, onto cookie sheet and return to oven 5 to 10 minutes to dry out. Remove to wire rack to cool completely.

Prepare pastry cream. In the top of a double boiler over low heat, melt chocolate, stirring until smooth. Set aside. In a saucepan over medium heat, bring milk to a boil. In a bowl, beat egg yolks and sugar until pale and thick, 3 to 5 minutes. Stir in flour just until blended.

Slowly pour about 1 cup hot milk into egg yolks, stirring constantly. Return yolk mixture to pan and cook over medium heat about 1 minute, until sauce thickens and boils, stirring constantly; remove from heat and quickly stir in melted chocolate until well blended. Strain into a large bowl and place a piece of plastic wrap directly against surface of cream to prevent a skin forming. Cool to room temperature. Carefully peel plastic wrap from cooled pastry cream. Fold in whipped cream.

Spoon cream into a large pastry bag fitted with a large star or plain tip. Fill each puff bottom with pastry cream and cover each puff with its top. Arrange cream puffs on a large serving plate in a single layer or pile them on top of each other.

To serve, in a saucepan over low heat, melt chocolate and butter with cream until well blended. Remove from heat and cool 10 to 15 minutes, until slightly thickened. Pour sauce over cream puffs and serve while chocolate sauce is still warm.

DOUBLE-CHOCOLATE BERRY TART WITH BLACKBERRY SAUCE

10–12 SERVINGS

This tart looks spectacular. It is worth searching for blackberries, boysenberries and loganberries when in season as they really do look and taste dramatic with the chocolate. Raspberries and blueberries can be used if other berries are unavailable.

½ cup (1 stick) butter, softened
½ cup superfine sugar
½ tsp. salt
1 tsp. vanilla extract
¾ cup unsweetened cocoa powder
1¼ cups all-purpose flour

CHOCOLATE GANACHE FILLING
2½ cups heavy cream
½ cup seedless blackberry preserves
8 squares (8 oz.) bittersweet chocolate, chopped
2 tbsp. butter, cut into pieces

BLACKBERRY SAUCE
8 oz. fresh or frozen blackberries or raspberries
1 tbsp. lemon juice
2 tbsp. sugar
2 tbsp. blackberry- or raspberry-flavor liqueur
1 lb. blackberries, loganberries and boysenberries, or any combination

Prepare pastry. In a food processor fitted with metal blade, process the butter, sugar, salt and vanilla until creamy. Add the cocoa powder and process 1 minute, until well blended; scrape side of bowl. Add flour all at once and using the *pulse action,* process 10 to 15 seconds, just until blended.

Place a piece of plastic wrap on work surface. Turn out dough onto plastic wrap. Use plastic wrap to help shape dough into flat disk and wrap tightly. Refrigerate 1 hour.

Lightly grease a 9-in. tart pan with removable bottom. Soften dough 5 to 10 minutes, at room temperature. Roll out dough between 2 sheets of waxed paper or plastic wrap to an 11-in. circle about ¼-in. thick. Peel off top sheet of plastic wrap and invert dough into prepared pan. Ease dough into pan. Remove plastic wrap.

With floured fingers, press dough onto bottom and side of pan, then roll rolling pin over pan edge to cut off any excess dough. Prick bottom of dough with fork. Refrigerate 1 hour.

Preheat oven to 375°F. Line tart shell with foil or parchment paper; fill with dry beans or rice. Bake 10 minutes; lift out foil with beans and bake 5 minutes longer, just until set. Pastry may look underdone on the bottom, it will dry out. Remove to wire rack to cool completely.

Prepare filling. In a saucepan over medium heat, bring cream and blackberry preserves to a boil. Remove from heat and add chocolate all at once, stirring until melted and smooth. Stir in butter, then strain into cooled tart, tilting tart to evenly distribute filling. Cool tart completely.

Prepare sauce. In a food processor, combine blackberries, lemon juice and sugar and process until smooth. Strain into a small bowl and add blackberry-flavor liqueur. If sauce is too thick, thin with a little water.

To serve, arrange the berries on the top of the tart. With a pastry brush, brush berries with a little blackberry sauce to glaze lightly. Serve remaining sauce separately with tart.

SWEET SUCCESS

This chocolate pastry has a cookie-like texture and is difficult to handle. If you find it too soft to roll, place the dough into the pan and use lightly floured fingers to press the dough into the bottom and up the side of the pan.

BLACK-BOTTOM LEMON TARTLETS

MAKEES 12

The dark chocolate surprise beneath the creamy lemon custard is the black bottom in these flaky tartlet shells. Serve them on their own or more dramatically on a pool of chocolate-dotted lemon-custard sauce.

1½ cups all-purpose flour
2 tbsp. confectioners' sugar
½ tsp. salt
¾ cup (1½ sticks) unsalted butter, cut into pieces and at room temperature
1 egg yolk
½ tsp. vanilla extract
2–3 tbsp. cold water

LEMON CUSTARD SAUCE
1 lemon
1½ cups milk
6 egg yolks
⅓ cup sugar

LEMON CURD FILLING
2 lemons
¾ cup (1½ sticks) unsalted butter, cut into pieces
1 cup sugar
3 eggs

CHOCOLATE FILLING
¾ cup cream
6 squares (6 oz.) bittersweet or semisweet chocolate, chopped
2 tbsp. unsalted butter, cut into pieces
Chocolate Triangles (see Decorating with Chocolate) for garnish
1 square (1 oz.) bittersweet or semisweet chocolate, melted

Prepare custard sauce. With a swivel-bladed vegetable peeler, remove strips of zest from lemon. Place in a medium saucepan over medium heat with the milk and bring to a boil. Remove from heat and leave 5 minutes to infuse. Reheat milk gently.

With an electric mixer, beat egg yolks and sugar until pale and thick, 2 to 3 minutes. Pour about 1 cup hot milk over, beating vigorously. Return egg-yolk mixture to pan and cook gently over low heat, stirring constantly with a wooden spoon until mixture thickens and lightly coats the back of the spoon; do not let boil or it will curdle. Strain into a chilled bowl. Squeeze 2 tbsp. juice from the lemon and stir into sauce. Cool; stirring occasionally. Refrigerate until ready to use.

Prepare lemon curd filling. Grate the zest and squeeze the juice of the lemons into the top of a double boiler. Add butter and sugar and stir over medium heat until the butter is melted and sugar dissolved. Lower heat. In a bowl, lightly beat the eggs, then strain into butter mixture. Cook over low heat, stirring constantly with a wooden spoon until mixture thickens and coats the back of the spoon, about 15 minutes. Pour (or strain if you do not want the lemon zest) into a bowl. Cool, stirring occasionally. Refrigerate to thicken.

Prepare pastry. Place flour, sugar and salt into a food processor fitted with metal blade. Process to blend. Add butter and process 15 to 20 seconds, until mixture resembles coarse crumbs. In a bowl, beat the yolk with the vanilla and water. With machine running, pour yolk mixture through feed tube just until dough begins to stick together; *do not allow dough to form a ball* or pastry will be tough. If dough appears too dry add 1 to 2 tbsp. more cold water, little by little, just until dough holds together.

Place a piece of plastic wrap on a work surface. Turn dough out onto plastic wrap. Use plastic wrap to help shape dough into a flat disk. Wrap tightly and refrigerate at least 30 minutes.

Lightly butter twelve 3-in. tartlet pans (if possible, with removable bottoms). On a lightly floured surface, roll out pastry to an oblong shape slightly more than ⅛-in. thick. Using a 4-in. fluted cutter, cut out 12 circles and press each one onto bottom and side of tartlet pans. Prick bottom of dough with a fork. Place pans on a large cookie sheet and refrigerate 30 minutes.

Preheat oven to 375°F. Cut out twelve 5-in. circles of foil and line each pan; fill with dry beans or rice. Bake 5 to 8 minutes; remove foil with beans and bake 5 minutes longer, until golden. Remove tartlets to wire rack to cool.

Prepare chocolate filling. In a saucepan over medium heat, bring cream to a boil. Remove from heat and stir in chocolate all at once until melted and smooth. Beat in butter and leave to cool slightly.

Spoon an equal amount of chocolate filling into each tartlet to cover bottom and make a layer about ¼-in. thick. Refrigerate 10 minutes to allow chocolate layer to set.

Onto each chocolate-filled tartlet, spoon over a layer of lemon curd to come just to the top of the pastry. Set aside, but do not refrigerate or chocolate layer will be too firm.

Spoon a little custard onto dessert plate. Remove tartlet from pan and place in center of plate. Decorate each tartlet with a chocolate triangle. If you like, spoon melted chocolate into a paper cone (see Decorating with Chocolate), cut ⅛-in. opening and make drops of chocolate in a circle 1 in. from the edge of plate. Draw a toothpick or skewer through chocolate to marble into the custard or make "heart" motif.

SWEET SUCCESS

Pastry and tartlets can be prepared a day ahead. These tartlets are best filled just a few hours before serving so fillings are still soft.

An easy way to blind bake tartlets is to use cupcake liners. One small liner just covers the bottom and side of a 3-in. tartlet mold.

Desserts

HOT CHOCOLATE SOUFFLÉ WITH WHITE CHOCOLATE AND ORANGE SAUCE

6 SERVINGS

This elegant dessert is surprisingly simple to make, and, although it must be served immediately when baked, it can be prepared several hours ahead, leaving only the egg whites to be beaten and folded in at the last moment. The extra chocolate sauce is optional.

granulated sugar for sprinkling dish
4 squares (4 oz.) bittersweet or semisweet chocolate, chopped
1/4 cup (1/2 stick) unsalted butter, cut into pieces
4 eggs, separated
2 tbsp. orange-flavor liqueur
1/4 tsp. cream of tartar
2 tbsp. sugar
confectioners' sugar for dusting

CHOCOLATE AND ORANGE SAUCE
3 oz. fine-quality white chocolate, chopped
1/3 cup whipping cream
2 tbsp. orange-flavor liqueur
2 tbsp. orange juice

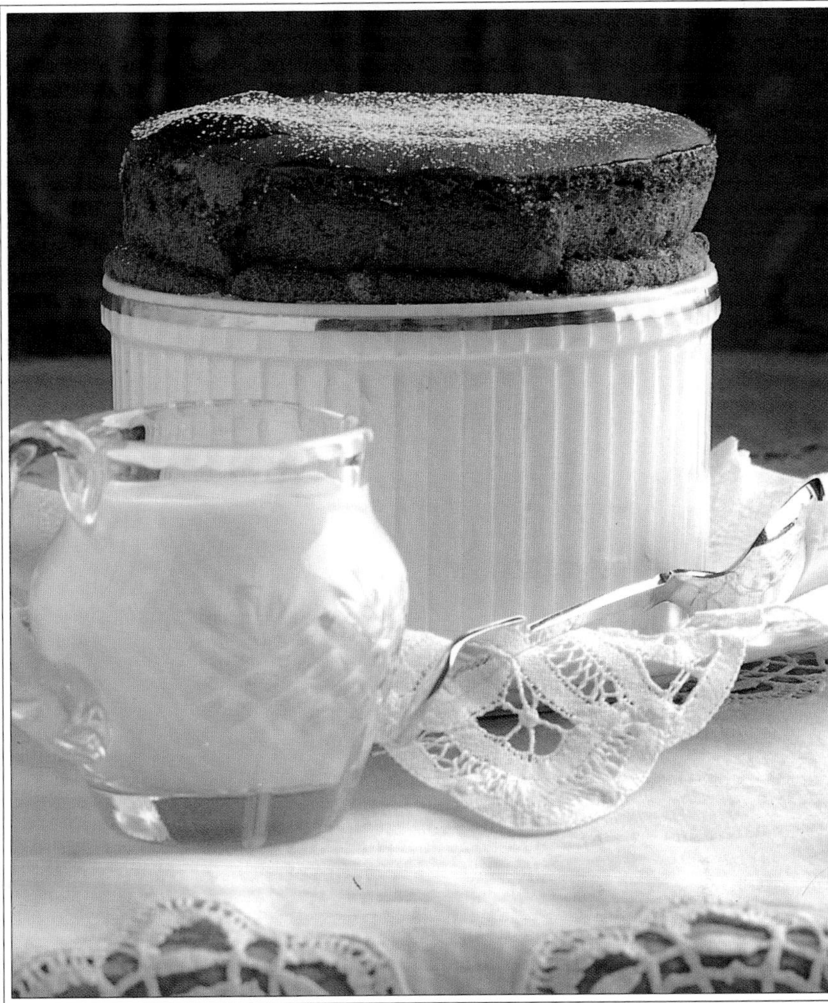

Preheat oven to 475°F. Generously butter bottom and side of a 4-cup soufflé dish. Refrigerate 5 minutes to set butter, then re-butter dish. Lightly sprinkle bottom and side of dish with sugar, then shake out any excess.

In a saucepan over low heat, melt the chocolate and butter, stirring frequently until smooth. Remove from heat. Beat in egg yolks and orange-flavor liqueur. Set aside to cool slightly, stirring occasionally.

With electric mixer, beat egg whites and cream of tartar together until stiff peaks form. Sprinkle sugar over and continue beating 1 minute, until sugar is incorporated and whites are glossy.

Fold one-quarter of beaten whites into cooled chocolate mixture to lighten, then fold in remaining whites. Do not overwork mixture; it is better to have a few streaks of white than to deflate the mixture. Pour into the prepared dish.

Place on a cookie sheet and bake 5 minutes. Reduce temperature to 425°F and bake 10 to 12 minutes longer. Top of soufflé should be set but the soufflé should jiggle when cookie sheet is moved; it should remain soft in the center.

Meanwhile, prepare sauce. In a saucepan over low heat, melt chocolate with cream, stirring frequently until smooth. Stir in orange-flavor liqueur and juice. Strain into sauceboat and set aside to keep warm.

To serve, fold a dinner napkin or doily on a serving plate to prevent soufflé from sliding on plate. Dust top of soufflé with confectioners' sugar. Transfer from cookie sheet to prepared serving plate. Serve soufflé immediately; pass sauce separately.

SWEET SUCCESS

To serve a soufflé "French-style," use a serving spoon to "crack" the top, much like cracking a soft-boiled egg. Serve some of the firmer outside and the softer center to each guest and pass any sauce separately.

Soufflés make a spectacular presentation when served in individual dishes. Prepare six 2/3-cup ramekins as directed, but bake 10 to 12 minutes at 425°F.

CHOCOLATE CRÊPES WITH PINEAPPLE AND BITTER CHOCOLATE SAUCE

MAKES 12 CREPES

The combination of chocolate and pineapple is delicious. The addition of chocolate chips and toasted macadamias adds texture and flavor when the crêpes are heated. Serve with the hot, bitter chocolate sauce.

7 tbsp. all-purpose flour
1 tbsp. unsweetened cocoa powder
1 tsp. sugar
¼ tsp. salt
2 eggs
¾ cup milk
2 tbsp. unsalted butter, melted, plus extra for reheating crêpes
1 tsp. vanilla extract
vegetable oil for greasing pan

PINEAPPLE FILLING

1 pineapple, peeled, cored and cut into ½-in. pieces or 1 16-oz. can pineapple pieces in juice, drained
2 tbsp. unsalted butter
½ tsp. ground cinnamon
¼ cup natural maple syrup
⅓ cup bittersweet, semisweet or milk chocolate chips
⅓ cup macadamia nuts, chopped and toasted (2 oz.)

CHOCOLATE SAUCE

3 squares (3 oz.) bittersweet or semisweet chocolate, chopped
1 square (1 oz.) unsweetened chocolate, chopped
⅓ cup water
3 tbsp. natural maple syrup
2 tbsp. unsalted butter, cut into pieces
confectioners' sugar for dusting
fresh cranberries or raspberries and mint leaves for garnish

Into a bowl, sift flour, cocoa powder, sugar and salt. Mix to blend; make a well in center.

In another bowl, lightly beat the eggs with the milk. Gradually add to the well in the center of flour mixture. Using a whisk, blend in flour from sides of bowl to form a paste, then a batter; beat until smooth. Stir in melted butter and vanilla and strain into another bowl. Leave to stand 1 hour.

With a pastry brush, brush the bottom of a 7- or 8-in. crêpe pan or skillet with a little vegetable oil. Heat pan over medium heat. Stir batter (if batter is too thick, stir in a little milk or water; it should be thin). Fill a ¼-cup measure or small ladle three-quarters full with batter, then pour into hot pan. Quickly tilt and rotate pan to cover bottom of pan with a thin layer of batter. Cook over medium-high heat 1 to 2 minutes, until top is set and bottom is golden. With a metal spatula, loosen edge of crêpe from pan, turn over and cook 30 to 45 seconds, just until set. Turn out onto plate.

Continue making crêpes, stirring batter occasionally and brushing pan lightly with oil. (A nonstick pan is ideal and does not need additional greasing.) Stack crêpes with sheets of waxed paper between each. Set aside.

Prepare filling. In a large skillet over medium-high heat, melt butter until sizzling. Add pineapple pieces and sauté until golden, 3 to 4 minutes. Sprinkle with cinnamon and stir in maple syrup. Cook 1 to 2 minutes longer, until pineapple is lightly coated with syrup and liquid has evaporated. Remove from heat.

Lay a crêpe on a plate or work surface, bottom side down. Spoon a little pineapple mixture onto top half of crêpe. Sprinkle over a few chocolate chips and macadamia nuts. Fold bottom half over, then fold into quarters. Continue using all the crêpes, pineapple filling, chocolate chips and nuts. Set each one on a buttered cookie sheet and cover tightly with foil until ready to serve.

Prepare chocolate sauce. In a medium saucepan over low heat, melt chocolate with water and maple syrup, stirring frequently until smooth and well blended. Stir in butter. Keep warm.

Preheat oven to 375°F. Uncover crêpes, brush top of each with melted butter and re-cover tightly. Bake 5 minutes just until heated through. Place on a dessert plate or individual plates. Dust with confectioners' sugar and garnish with fresh cranberries or raspberries and mint leaves. Serve chocolate sauce separately.

TRUFFLE-FILLED POACHED PEARS

6 SERVINGS

These richly colored port-poached pears are filled with a luscious chocolate-truffle surprise. For a really full flavor, the pears should be poached a day ahead and left to soak up the port syrup overnight.

thinly pared strips of zest and juice of 1 lemon
thinly pared strips of zest and juice of 1 orange
1 cinnamon stick
4–5 whole cloves
½ bottle tawny port wine
½ cup sugar
½ cup red currant jelly or seedless raspberry preserves
2–3 cups water
6 firm pears, all the same size

CHOCOLATE TRUFFLE FILLING
3 tbsp. whipping cream
¼ cup reserved poaching syrup
6 squares (6 oz.) bittersweet or semisweet chocolate, chopped
2 tbsp. unsalted butter, cut into pieces
Chocolate Leaves (see Decorating with Chocolate) for garnish

In a saucepan large enough to hold pears in a single layer, combine lemon and orange zests and juices, cinnamon stick, cloves, port wine, sugar, red currant jelly and water; there should be enough liquid to cover pears. Bring to a boil, boil 1 to 2 minutes, then lower heat to a simmer.

Slice bottom from each pear so it stands flat. With a swivel-bladed vegetable peeler, peel pears and core from bottom end leaving stem attached. Drop pears into poaching syrup and cover with a circle of waxed paper with a slit made in the center (this keeps pears under the liquid). Bring pears to a boil, then reduce heat to low and simmer 15 to 20 minutes, just until tender or when sharp knife enters flesh easily. Remove from heat and cool pears in poaching liquid, 3 to 4 hours.

Transfer pears from liquid to a large bowl. Bring syrup to a boil and reduce 20 minutes over high heat, until syrup is thickened and coats the back of a spoon lightly. Strain over pears and leave to cool to room temperature. Refrigerate overnight.

Prepare chocolate filling. In a saucepan over medium heat, bring cream and poaching syrup to a boil. Add chocolate, stirring until melted and smooth. Beat in butter. Refrigerate 1 hour, until chocolate is thick enough to pipe.

Remove pears from their liquid to wire rack placed over a cookie sheet to catch any drips. Spoon chocolate into medium pastry bag fitted with medium plain tip and gently pipe chocolate mixture into center of pears. Reserve any left over chocolate. Stand each pear on a plate.

To serve, pour a little poaching syrup onto one side of each plate. Gently reheat any left over chocolate-truffle mixture and spoon a little over each pear. Garnish each pear with a chocolate leaf near stem. Place other leaves on plate if you like.

SWEET SUCCESS

It is best to poach pears 1 day ahead or at least early on the day of serving so the pears have a chance to cool and absorb the poaching liquid. They should have an almost translucent quality and the syrup should be thickened to a glazing consistency.

CHOCOLATE PAVLOVA WITH KIWIFRUIT AND ORANGE

8 TO 10 SERVINGS

Both Australia and New Zealand claim to have invented this delicate meringue-based dessert, named for the ballerina Anna Pavlova. I have added cocoa powder to the meringue, filled it with chocolate cream and topped it with a mixture of fruits, tiny wallflowers and herbs.

3 tbsp. unsweetened cocoa powder
1 tsp. cornstarch
4 egg whites, at room temperature
1/4 tsp. salt
1 cup superfine sugar
1 tsp. cider vinegar

WHITE CHOCOLATE CREAM
4 oz. good-quality white chocolate, chopped
1/2 cup milk
1 tbsp. unsalted butter, cut into pieces
1/3 cup confectioners' sugar, sifted
1 cup heavy cream
2 kiwifruits, peeled and sliced
2 cups orange segments
fresh mint sprigs for garnish
wallflowers

Preheat oven to 325°F. Place a sheet of nonstick parchment paper on a large cookie sheet and mark an 8-in. circle on it using a plate or cake pan as a guide. Into a bowl, sift together cocoa powder and cornstarch; set aside.

In another bowl with electric mixer, beat egg whites until frothy. Add salt and continue beating until stiff peaks form. Sprinkle in sugar, 1 tbsp. at a time, making sure each addition is well blended before adding the next, until stiff and glossy. Fold in cocoa and cornstarch mixture, then fold in vinegar.

Spoon mixture onto the circle on the paper, spreading the meringue evenly and building up the sides higher than the center. Bake in center of oven 45–50 minutes, until set. Turn off the oven and leave meringue to stand in the oven 45 minutes longer, the meringue may crack or sink.

Meanwhile, prepare chocolate cream. In a saucepan over low heat, melt chocolate with milk, stirring until smooth. Beat in butter and cool completely.

Remove meringue from oven. Using a metal spatula, transfer to a serving plate. Cut a circle around center of meringue about 2 in. from edge; this allows the center to sink gently without pulling the edges in.

When the chocolate mixture is completely cooled, in a bowl with electric mixer, beat cream until soft peaks form. Stir half the cream into the chocolate to lighten, then fold in remaining cream. Spoon into center of meringue.

Arrange kiwifruit and orange in center over the chocolate cream and garnish with fresh mint and wallflowers.

VARIATION

For a more elegant presentation, pipe meringue mixture into a 9-in. round using a large star tip.

APRICOT-GLAZED WHITE CHOCOLATE RICE PUDDING WITH BITTER CHOCOLATE SAUCE

10 SERVINGS

The addition of white chocolate to rice pudding transforms a homely dessert into an elegant one. The apricot glaze and chocolate sauce are the perfect foil to the sweet, creamy pudding. Soak the raisins overnight for the fullest flavor.

¾ cup golden raisins
3 tbsp. hot water
2 tbsp. apricot brandy or orange-flavor liqueur
1 cup medium- or long-grain white rice
1½ cups milk
1 cup water
2 tbsp. butter
½ cup sugar
6 oz. fine-quality white chocolate, chopped
3 eggs
2 cups heavy cream
2 tsp. vanilla extract
1 teaspoon ground cinnamon
½ teaspoon grated nutmeg

APRICOT GLAZE

½ cup apricot preserves
1 tbsp. orange juice or water
1 tbsp. apricot brandy or orange-flavor liqueur

BITTER CHOCOLATE SAUCE

¾ cup heavy cream
¼ cup sugar
¾ cup apricot preserves
4 squares (4 oz.) unsweetened chocolate, chopped
2 squares (2 oz.) bittersweet or semisweet chocolate, chopped
2 tbsp. apricot brandy or orange-flavor liqueur

In a bowl, combine raisins, hot water and apricot brandy. Leave to stand at least 2 hours.

In a heavy bottomed saucepan, combine rice, 1 cup milk, water, butter and ¼ cup sugar. Bring to a boil, stirring occasionally. Reduce heat, cover and simmer 18 to 20 minutes, just until liquid is absorbed.

Meanwhile, preheat oven to 300°F. Butter a 6- to 8-cup shallow baking dish or soufflé dish and set aside. In a saucepan over low heat, melt chocolate with remaining ½ cup milk, stirring frequently until smooth. Remove from heat. In a large bowl, lightly beat eggs, remaining sugar, cream, vanilla, cinnamon and nutmeg. Slowly beat in melted chocolate until well blended. Stir in the raisins and any liquid. Stir egg mixture into cooked rice mixture until well blended, then pour into baking dish. Cover with foil.

Set baking dish into a roasting pan. Fill pan with hot water to about halfway up the side of the dish. Bake 30 minutes, uncover and bake 15 to 20 minutes longer, until a knife inserted 2 ins. from the edge of dish comes out clean; center should remain slightly moist. Run sharp knife around edge of dish to loosen pudding from edge and prevent center from splitting. Leave to cool 1 hour.

Meanwhile, prepare glaze. In a saucepan over medium heat, melt apricot preserves with orange juice and apricot brandy, stirring until smooth. Gently spoon over top of pudding to glaze.

Prepare chocolate sauce. In a saucepan over low heat, bring cream, sugar and apricot preserves to a boil. Remove from the heat and stir in both chocolates all at once until melted and smooth. Press through a strainer and stir in apricot brandy; keep warm. Serve with glazed rice pudding.

SWEET SUCCESS

This pudding can be made in individual molds and unmolded for a more elegant presentation. Butter ten ⅔-cup custard cups or ramekins and line bottom of each with waxed or parchment paper. Butter paper. Bake 3–5 minutes less than for above recipe. Cool puddings at least 1 hour; do not glaze. Unmold each pudding onto a plate, remove paper and top with a little warm glaze; spread evenly. Pour over a little chocolate sauce and serve remainder separately.

CHOCOLATE TIRAMISÙ

14 TO 16 SERVINGS

A classic Italian dessert which has become so popular everywhere there must be hundreds of variations. This one combines chocolate with the traditional coffee flavor and does not use any uncooked eggs in the creamy filling so it can be prepared days ahead. It should be soft but firm enough to slice and hold its shape.

CHOCOLATE LADYFINGERS

2/3 cup plus 2 tbsp. all-purpose flour
1/4 cup unsweetened cocoa powder
1 tbsp. instant espresso or coffee powder
1/4 tsp. salt
4 eggs, separated
1/2 cup superfine sugar
2 tsp. vanilla extract
1/4 tsp. cream of tartar
confectioners' sugar for dusting

CHOCOLATE MASCARPONE FILLING

1 17 1/2-oz. container mascarpone cheese, at room temperature
1/2 cup confectioners' sugar, sifted
1 1/2 cups freshly brewed expresso or instant coffee
2 1/2 cups heavy cream
6 squares (6 oz.) bittersweet or semisweet chocolate, melted and cooled
6 tbsp. coffee-flavor liqueur
2 squares (2 oz.) bittersweet or semisweet chocolate, grated
2 tbsp. chocolate-flavor liqueur
cocoa powder for dusting
whipped cream for garnish (optional)

Prepare ladyfingers. Grease 2 large cookie sheets. Line with waxed or parchment paper. Grease and lightly flour paper. In a bowl, sift together *twice* flour, cocoa powder, espresso powder and salt. Mix well and set aside.

In another bowl with electric mixer, beat egg yolks with 1/4 cup sugar until thick and pale, 2 to 3 minutes. Beat in vanilla.

In a large bowl with electric mixer and cleaned beaters, beat egg whites and cream of tartar until stiff peaks form. Sprinkle over remaining sugar, 2 tbsp. at a time, beating well after each addition.

Fold 1 spoonful egg whites into egg-yolk mixture to lighten, then fold in remaining whites. Sift flour mixture over and fold into yolk-white mixture, but do not overwork mixture. Spoon batter into a large pastry bag fitted with a medium (about 1/2-in.) plain tip. Pipe batter into about thirty 5-in. or twenty-four 4-in. ladyfingers. Dust with confectioners' sugar.

Bake 12 to 15 minutes, until set and tops feel firm when touched with a fingertip. Remove to wire rack to cool on pans 10 minutes. With a wide spatula, remove ladyfingers to wire racks to cool completely.

With hand-held electric mixer at low speed, beat mascarpone cheese with confectioners' sugar just until smooth. Gradually beat in 1/4 cup espresso or coffee powder; do not overbeat.

In another bowl with electric mixer, beat cream until soft peaks form. Gently fold cream into mascarpone mixture. Divide mixture in half. Fold melted chocolate and 2 tbsp. coffee-flavor liqueur into half until blended. Fold grated chocolate and chocolate-flavor liqueur into remaining mascarpone mixture. Set both mixtures aside.

Into a bowl or pie plate wide enough to hold the ladyfingers, combine *half* the remaining espresso coffee with 2 tbsp. coffee-flavor liqueur. Quickly dip one side of a ladyfinger into coffee mixture and place it dry-side down in a 13- × 9-in. baking dish; do not let ladyfingers get too soggy or they may fall apart. Continue with about half the ladyfingers (you will need enough for 2 layers) to form a fairly close layer with not much space between each ladyfinger. Drizzle over remaining espresso mixture. Place remaining espresso- and 2 tbsp. coffee-flavor liqueur into pie plate.

Pour chocolate-mascarpone mixture over the bottom layer of ladyfingers smoothing the chocolate mixture. Layer remaining ladyfingers over the chocolate layers, dipping each one into the espresso mixture 1 at a time. Drizzle over any remaining expresso mixture. Pour remaining grated chocolate-mascarpone mixture over this layer and smooth the top leaving no spaces between filling and sides of dish. Cover dish tightly and refrigerate overnight. Dust top with cocoa powder before serving. If you like, decorate with extra whipped cream.

SWEET SUCCESS

Mascarpone is an Italian cream cheese with a smooth creamy texture and soft, sweet flavor. It is available from supermarkets, Italian markets and specialty stores in 17 1/2-oz. containers. A quicker version can be made using about 7 oz. bought ladyfingers or a 7-oz. package of imported ladyfingers called savoiardi cookies. In any case, make this dessert at least 1 day ahead to allow the mixture to set firm and the flavors to mingle.

TRIPLE CHOCOLATE MOUSSE PARFAITS

6 SERVINGS

This trio of delicate chocolate mousses is served in sundae, parfait or wine glasses to show off the layers. It could be equally impressive layered into a larger straight-sided glass bowl—either way, it is worth the effort. These can be made one to two days ahead and stored in the refrigerator, covered with plastic wrap.

BITTERSWEET CHOCOLATE MOUSSE

4 squares (4 oz.) bittersweet chocolate, chopped
¼ cup whipping cream
1 tbsp. unsalted butter, cut into pieces
2 eggs, separated
1 tbsp. rum
⅛ tsp. cream of tartar

MILK CHOCOLATE MOUSSE

4 oz. fine-quality milk chocolate, chopped
¼ cup whipping cream
2 tbsp. unsalted butter, cut into pieces
2 eggs, separated
1 tbsp. coffee-flavor liqueur
⅛ tsp. cream of tartar

WHITE CHOCOLATE MOUSSE

4 oz. fine-quality white chocolate, chopped
¼ cup whipping cream
1 tbsp. unsalted butter, cut into pieces
2 eggs, separated
1 tbsp. chocolate-flavor liqueur
⅛ tsp. cream of tartar
6 tbsp. chocolate syrup
1 cup whipped cream for garnish
6 chocolate coffee beans

Prepare bittersweet chocolate mousse. In a saucepan, melt chocolate with cream, stirring frequently until smooth. Remove from heat. Stir in butter and beat in egg yolks, 1 at a time, then stir in rum. Allow to cool.

With electric mixer, beat whites and cream of tartar until stiff peaks form; do not overbeat. Stir in 1 spoonful of whites into the chocolate mixture to lighten, then fold in remaining whites.

Using a ladle or tablespoon, carefully spoon an equal amount of mousse into each of 6 sundae, parfait or wine glasses. Do not touch edge of glass; if any of the mixture drips, wipe glass clean. Place glasses on a tray or cookie sheet and refrigerate 1 hour, or until firmly set.

Prepare milk chocolate mousse as above, then spoon equal amounts over bittersweet chocolate mousse. Refrigerate about 1 hour, until set.

Prepare white chocolate mousse as above, then spoon equal amounts over the milk chocolate mousse. Cover each glass with plastic wrap and refrigerate 4 to 6 hours or overnight, until set.

To serve, spoon 1 tbsp. chocolate syrup over each mousse. Spoon whipped cream into a small pastry bag fitted with a medium star tip and pipe a rosette of cream onto each mousse. Garnish with chocolate coffee beans.

WHITE CHOCOLATE FRUIT FOOLS IN CHOCOLATE CUPS

12 SERVINGS

Fruit fools are a dessert made from a fruit purée folded into whipped cream. This elegant version combines white chocolate mousse and three fruit purées presented in chocolate cups. Use any fruit combination you like.

12 Chocolate Cups (see Decorating with Chocolate)

MANGO PURÉE

1 mango, peeled and cut into cubes (about 1½ cups), with 4 cubes reserved for garnish
grated zest and juice of ½ orange
1 tsp. lemon juice or to taste
1 tbsp. sugar or to taste

KIWIFRUIT PURÉE

3 kiwifruits, peeled and sliced with 4 slices reserved for garnish
grated zest of 1 lime with 1–2 tsp. juice
1 tbsp. sugar or to taste

CRANBERRY-RASPBERRY PURÉE

⅔ cup fresh raspberries with berries reserved for garnish
1 tbsp. lemon juice
1 tsp. sugar or to taste
½ 16-oz. can whole-berry cranberry sauce

WHITE CHOCOLATE MOUSSE

4 oz. fine-quality white chocolate, chopped
¼ cup milk
1 tbsp. orange-flavor liqueur
1¼ cups heavy cream
2 egg whites
¼ tsp. cream of tartar

Prepare chocolate cups as directed on page 11, using 24 squares (1½ lbs.) semisweet chocolate and 1 tbsp. vegetable shortening and extra large muffin-pan liners.

Prepare fruit purées in a food processor or blender, beginning with the lightest color purée to avoid washing the processor after each purée. Place mango cubes in the processor with orange zest and juice. Process until smooth. Taste purée and add lemon juice and sugar if necessary; this depends on the natural sweetness of the fruit. Scrape purée into a bowl. Cover and refrigerate.

Place kiwifruit slices into the processor with lime zest and juice. Process until smooth. Taste purée and add more lime juice and sugar if necessary. Scrape purée into a bowl. Cover and refrigerate.

Place the raspberries, lemon juice and sugar into the food processor. Process until smooth. Press through a strainer into a bowl. Return to food processor. Add the cranberry sauce and using the *pulse action*, process once or twice, just to blend, but leaving some texture to the purée. Taste purée and add more lemon juice or sugar if necessary. Scrape purée into small bowl. Cover and refrigerate.

Prepare mousse. In a saucepan over low heat, melt white chocolate with milk, stirring frequently until smooth. Remove from heat and stir in orange-flavor liqueur. Cool to room temperature.

With hand-held electric mixer, beat cream until soft peaks form. Stir 1 spoonful of cream into chocolate mixture to lighten, then fold in remaining cream.

In another bowl with electric mixer with clean beaters, beat egg whites and cream of tartar until stiff peaks form. Fold into chocolate-cream mixture. (You may not want to use *all* the egg whites if the mousse is soft enough; this depends on the brand of chocolate used.) Divide into 3 bowls.

To assemble, arrange the prepared chocolate cups on 1 large or 2 smaller cookie sheets (arrange adequate refrigerator space beforehand). Spoon a little of the mango purée into 4 chocolate cups. Spoon a little of the raspberry into 4 of the chocolate cups and then the kiwifruit purée into the remaining 4 cups. Reserve a little of each purée for topping, then fold each of the purées into one of each of the 3 bowls of mousse; *do not mix well*, leaving swirls of purée visible for effect. Spoon each fool mixture into the appropriate chocolate cups and top each with a decorative swirl of its matching purée. Refrigerate until ready to serve. Garnish each with a berry, cube or slice of fruit. Refrigerate at least 30 minutes or until firm.

SWEET SUCCESS

Pretty chocolate cups can be made using brioche molds or teacups. Line each mold or cup with a square of foil. Do not press tightly but allow it to form folds or soft pleats against the side of the mold or cup; be sure the bottom is flat. Spoon melted chocolate down the inside of the folds using a zig-zag motion and turning the cup. This gives an uneven pleated look.

WHITE CHOCOLATE FRUIT FOOLS IN CHOCOLATE CUPS

CHOCOLATE-RASPBERRY CHARLOTTE

8–10 SERVINGS

This creamy chocolate-raspberry charlotte is easy to make, but stunning enough for a very special occasion. Tie a satin ribbon around the ladyfingers before serving for an unusual presentation.

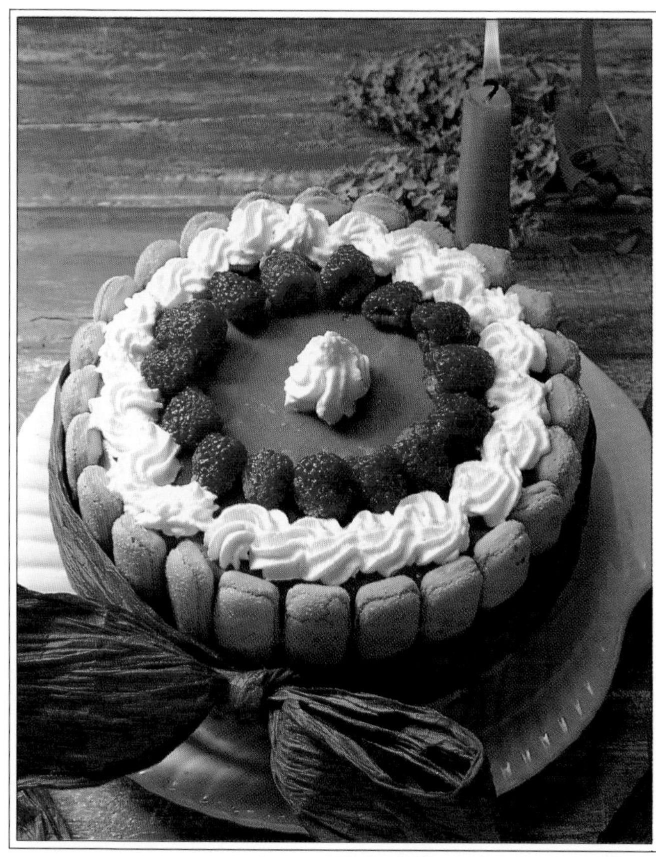

vegetable oil for pan
2 3½-oz. packages ladyfingers
1 10-oz. package frozen raspberries in light syrup, defrosted
½ cup seedless raspberry preserves
12 squares (12 oz.) bittersweet or semisweet chocolate, chopped
¼ cup raspberry-flavor liqueur
¼ cup water
2 eggs, separated, plus 2 whites
¼ tsp. cream of tartar
½ cup heavy cream
½ cup heavy cream, whipped, for garnish
1 ½-pt. container fresh raspberries for garnish

Lightly oil side of an 8-in. springform pan. Gently separate the ladyfingers lengthwise, but do not separate them if they are joined side-by-side. Trim bottom of the ladyfingers so they sit flat against the bottom of pan.

Line the side of the pan with ladyfingers, fitting tightly so no spaces exist. Line bottom of pan with remaining ladyfingers, cutting them to fit if necessary. Be sure there are not any spaces.

Drain frozen raspberries in a strainer. Into a saucepan, bring raspberry syrup and raspberry preserves to a boil. Boil 2 to 3 minutes, until sauce is thickened and syrupy. Remove from heat and cool slightly. With a pastry brush, brush ladyfingers on bottom of pan with syrup. Set aside.

In a saucepan over low heat, melt chocolate with raspberry-flavor liqueur and water, stirring frequently until smooth. Set aside. In a bowl, beat egg yolks 2 to 3 minutes, until pale and thick. Slowly beat in melted chocolate until well blended. Set aside.

In another bowl with hand-held electric mixer, beat cream until soft peaks form. Stir 1 spoonful of cream into chocolate mixture to lighten. Set remaining cream aside.

In another bowl with electric mixer, beat egg whites and cream of tartar until stiff peaks form. Gradually sprinkle sugar over, beating until sugar is dissolved and whites are glossy. Fold a large spoonful of whites into chocolate-cream mixture to lighten, then gently fold remaining whites and cream together until blended.

Spoon about one-third of the chocolate mixture into prepared pan, spreading it to the sides. Spoon the raspberries onto the chocolate half, spreading them evenly over the chocolate. Spoon in another third of the chocolate mixture, spreading it evenly. Top with remaining raspberries and cover completely with remaining chocolate mixture, smoothing the top evenly. Refrigerate 4 to 5 hours or overnight.

To serve, remove side of pan from charlotte. If necessary, use a thin-bladed knife to run between ladyfingers and side of pan. Transfer to a dessert plate.

Spoon whipped cream into a medium pastry bag fitted with a medium star tip. Pipe a circle of scrolls or rosettes around edge of charlotte close to ladyfingers. Garnish center of the charlotte with fresh raspberries and, if you like, tie a ribbon around finished dessert.

PEACHES N' WHITE CHOCOLATE CREAM MERINGUES

8 SERVINGS

This is a delicate combination of meringue, white chocolate cream and fragrant poached peaches.

MERINGUE SHELLS

3 egg whites
¼ tsp. cream of tartar
¾ cup superfine sugar
1 tsp. vanilla extract

POACHED PEACHES

½ cup sugar
½ cinnamon stick
2 strips zest from 1 lemon
3 cups water
4 large peaches, just ripe

WHITE CHOCOLATE CREAM

4 oz. fine-quality white chocolate, chopped
½ cup milk
1 tbsp. unsalted butter, cut into pieces
1 tbsp. vanilla extract or apricot brandy
1 cup heavy cream
lemon zest and mint leaves for garnish

Into a saucepan just large enough to hold the peaches, bring sugar, cinnamon stick, lemon zest and water to a boil; there should be enough liquid to cover peaches. Reduce heat.

Bring another saucepan about three-quarters full of water to a boil. Dip peaches into boiling water for 15 to 20 seconds, depending on ripeness. Transfer peaches to a bowl of ice water to cool. Remove from water and, using a small knife, carefully peel off skins. Alternatively, use a swivel-bladed vegetable peeler to peel peaches. Cut peaches in half lengthwise and, using a teaspoon, remove pits.

Drop peach halves into syrup and simmer 8 to 10 minutes, just until tender. Remove pan from the heat, but leave peaches to cool completely in syrup. Transfer peaches to a large bowl. Bring syrup to a boil and reduce until slightly thickened, 10 to 12 minutes. Strain syrup over peaches. Cool, then refrigerate until chilled, 2 to 3 hours.

Prepare meringue shells. Preheat oven to 275°F. Line a large cookie sheet with nonstick parchment paper or foil.

In a bowl with electric mixer, beat whites and cream of tartar until stiff peaks form. Gradually sprinkle three-quarters of the sugar over, a little at a time, beating well after each addition until whites are stiff and glossy. Fold in remaining sugar and vanilla.

Spoon mixture into a large pastry bag fitted with a medium star tip. Pipe eight 3-in. circles about 1½ in. apart onto cookie sheet. Pipe small rosettes in a ring around edge of each circle.

Bake 40 to 45 minutes, until set but not brown. Turn off oven and leave meringues in oven 45 minutes longer to dry out completely. Remove to wire rack to cool 10 minutes on cookie sheet. Then remove meringues from paper or foil to rack to cool completely. Store in an air-tight container if not using at once.

Prepare white chocolate cream. In a saucepan over low heat, melt white chocolate with milk, stirring frequently until smooth. Remove from heat and stir in butter and vanilla. Chill 1 hour.

With electric mixer, beat cream until soft peaks form; do not overbeat or mixture will be too firm. Stir 1 spoonful of cream into chocolate mixture to lighten, then fold in remaining cream. Chill until firm, about 1 hour.

Arrange meringue shells on a serving dish or individual plates. Fill each shell with white chocolate cream. Remove peaches from their syrup and pat dry with paper towels. Cut each peach half into thin slices and arrange over white chocolate cream. Garnish with lemon zest and mint leaves. Spoon a little syrup onto each plate or pass separately.

VELVETY CHOCOLATE MOUSSE

6 SERVINGS

Traditional chocolate mousse like the one found in little French bistros does not contain cream. I use it here to give the very dark chocolate an extra creamy texture—like velvet.

8 squares (8 oz.) bittersweet chocolate, chopped
2 tbsp. orange-flavor liqueur or brandy
¼ cup water
2 tbsp. unsalted butter, cut into pieces
3 eggs, separated
¼ tsp. cream of tartar
¼ cup sugar
½ cup whipping cream
whipping cream for garnish
orange slices for garnish

In a saucepan over low heat, melt chocolate with orange-flavor liqueur and water, stirring frequently until smooth. Remove from heat and beat in butter.

In a bowl, beat egg yolks until well blended. Beat into melted chocolate. Cool to room temperature.

With electric mixer, beat egg whites and cream of tartar until soft peaks form. Beat in sugar, 1 tbsp. at a time, beating well after each addition, until glossy but not too stiff or dry. Fold 1 large spoonful of whites into chocolate mixture to lighten.

In another bowl, whip cream until soft peaks form. Spoon cream over chocolate mixture and remaining whites over cream. Gently fold into chocolate just until blended. Pour into a serving bowl or into 6 individual dessert dishes and refrigerate at least 3 hours before serving. Garnish with whipped cream and sliced orange.

SWEET SUCCESS

Leave the chocolate mixture to cool sufficiently before adding the egg whites so that heat of the chocolate does not deflate the whites. Do not overfold the whites; it does not matter if a few white streaks remain.

VELVETY CHOCOLATE MOUSSE ►

CHOCOLATE BOX WITH WHITE CHOCOLATE MOUSSE AND BERRIES

8 SERVINGS

This dramatic dessert is much easier to make than it looks. The chocolate box can be made ahead and filled with any mousse; top with seasonal berries for a spectacular presentation.

CHOCOLATE BOX

6 squares (6 oz.) semisweet chocolate, chopped
1 tsp. vegetable shortening

WHITE CHOCOLATE MOUSSE

8 oz. fine-quality white chocolate, chopped
¼ cup milk
2 tbsp. cherry or orange-flavor liqueur
1½ cups heavy cream
2–3 egg whites, at room temperature
¼ tsp. cream of tartar

BERRY TOPPING

1 cup heavy cream (optional)
2–3 pts. (1½ lbs.) strawberries, cut in half or other mixed berries
fresh mint sprigs for garnish

Turn a 9-in. square cake pan upside down. Place a piece of foil over pan and press against bottom and sides of pan to make a square shape. Carefully remove foil from pan, turn pan right-side up and line pan with molded foil. Press foil against bottom and sides of pan smoothing out any wrinkles and folding any excess foil around pan edges.

In the top of a double boiler over low heat, melt chocolate and vegetable shortening, stirring frequently, until smooth. Pour onto the foil-lined pan and gently tilt pan to coat bottom and sides evenly. Refrigerate pan 1 minute, then swirl any remaining chocolate up sides of pan to reinforce sides of chocolate box. Refrigerate 30 to 40 minutes, until completely set.

Prepare mousse. In a saucepan over medium heat, melt chocolate with milk, stirring frequently until smooth. Remove from heat and stir in liqueur. Cool to room temperature.

With electric mixer, beat cream until soft peaks form, do not overwhip or the mousse will be too stiff. Stir half the cream into chocolate to lighten, then fold in remaining cream.

In a bowl with electric mixer and clean beaters, beat egg whites and cream of tartar until stiff peaks form. Fold into chocolate-cream mixture.

Remove chocolate box in foil from pan using foil as a guide. Gently peel foil from sides and base and place box on a serving plate. Spoon mousse into the box and spread evenly. Chill until firm, 2 to 3 hours.

Prepare topping. In a bowl with an electric mixer, beat cream until it forms soft peaks. Spoon into a large pastry bag fitted with a large star tip. Pipe a 1-in. border in a scroll or rosette pattern along sides of box. Fill center with strawberries, raspberries or mixed berries and decorate with mint sprigs.

FRUIT-STUDDED CHOCOLATE MARQUISE WITH BOURBON CUSTARD CREAM

12 TO 14 SERVINGS

Dried fruits such as raisins, apricots and prunes go so well with chocolate it was impossible to choose just one. This recipe combines three fruits in a dense, dark chocolate marquise mixture. This can be made several days ahead and stored in the refrigerator or even frozen.

⅓ cup golden raisins
⅓ cup chopped, pitted prunes
⅓ cup chopped, dried apricots
⅓ cup plus 1 tbsp. bourbon, Scotch whiskey or apricot brandy
12 squares (12 oz.) bittersweet chocolate, chopped
½ cup (1 stick) unsalted butter, cut into pieces
4 eggs, separated
¼ tsp. cream of tartar

BOURBON CUSTARD CREAM
2 cups half-and-half
2 large eggs
½ cup sugar
2 tbsp. bourbon, Scotch whiskey or apricot brandy

In a bowl, mix the raisins and dried fruit with bourbon. Leave to stand at least 2 hours, stirring occasionally.

Line a 9- × 5-in. loaf pan with plastic wrap, allowing enough wrap to fold over bottom when marquise is finished.

In a saucepan over low heat, melt chocolate and butter, stirring frequently until smooth. In a bowl with hand-held electric mixer, beat egg yolks until pale and thick, 3 to 4 minutes. Stir into warm chocolate mixture and cook over low heat 1 minute, stirring constantly until mixture thickens and looks shiny. Remove from heat and cool, stirring occasionally. Stir in fruit and any remaining bourbon.

With electric mixer, beat egg whites and cream of tartar until stiff peaks form; do not overbeat. Stir 1 large spoonful of whites into chocolate mixture to lighten, then fold in remaining whites.

Spoon into the pan. Chill just until firm, then fold over excess plastic wrap to cover the marquise. Refrigerate at least 6 hours or overnight.

Prepare bourbon cream. In a saucepan over medium heat, bring the half-and-half to a boil. Remove from heat. In a bowl, beat the eggs and sugar until well blended, about 1 minute.

Pour hot milk over and return mixture to saucepan over low heat. Cook 4 to 5 minutes, stirring constantly with a wooden spoon until mixture thickens and just coats the back of the spoon; do not boil or sauce will curdle. Strain into a chilled bowl and stir in bourbon. Refrigerate until ready to use.

To serve, slide marquise and its base onto a rectangular serving dish. Refrigerate until ready to serve. Cut into thin slices and serve with bourbon custard cream.

FRUITED WHITE CHOCOLATE BAVARIAN CREAMS WITH PASSION FRUIT AND CHOCOLATE SAUCES

8 SERVINGS

This gelatin-set white chocolate custard is made in heart-shaped molds for an effective presentation. It can be made easily in ramekins or in a larger pretty mold. Vary the fruits according to the season.

vegetable oil for molds
1 1/3 cups whipping cream
4 oz. fine-quality white chocolate, chopped
2 tsp. unflavored gelatin (2/3 package)
1/4 cup water
1 cup milk
4 egg yolks
1/4 cup sugar
2 tbsp. orange-flavor liqueur

PASSION FRUIT SAUCE

6 passion fruits or granadillas
1/4 cup orange juice
2 tbsp. sugar or to taste
1 tsp. cornstarch, dissolved in 1 tsp. water
1 tbsp. orange-flavor liqueur

CHOCOLATE-LIQUEUR SAUCE

8 squares (8 oz.) bittersweet chocolate, chopped
1/4 cup (1/2 stick) unsalted butter, cut into pieces
3/4 cup water
2–3 tablespoons chocolate-flavor liqueur
grated chocolate for garnish
fresh mint sprigs

Lightly oil 8 heart-shaped or other molds. In a saucepan over low heat, bring 1/3 cup cream to a boil. Add the white chocolate all at once, stirring until smooth. Set aside.

Sprinkle gelatin over water in a bowl; leave to stand and soften.

In a saucepan over medium heat, bring milk to a boil. In a bowl with a hand-held electric mixer, beat egg yolks and sugar until thick and pale, 2 to 3 minutes. Reduce mixer to lowest speed, gradually beat in milk, then return custard mixture to saucepan.

Cook custard over medium heat, stirring constantly with a wooden spoon until mixture thickens and coats the back of the spoon; do not boil or custard will curdle. Remove from the heat and stir in softened gelatin until dissolved, then stir into chocolate mixture. Strain custard into a large chilled bowl. Stir in orange-flavor liqueur and refrigerate about 20 minutes, until mixture begins to thicken.

In a bowl with electric mixer, beat remaining cream until soft peaks form. Gently fold into the thickening gelatin-custard mixture. Spoon an equal amount into each mold. Place molds on cookie sheet and refrigerate 2 hours, or until set. Cover all molds with plastic wrap and refrigerate several hours.

Prepare passion fruit sauce. Halve passion fruits or grandillas crosswise. Scoop juice and seeds into a saucepan. Stir in orange juice, sugar and dissolved cornstarch. Bring to a boil, then simmer 1 to 2 minutes, until sauce thickens. Remove from heat; cool slightly. Stir in orange-flavor liqueur.

Prepare chocolate sauce. In a saucepan over medium heat, melt chocolate and butter with water, stirring frequently until smooth. Remove from heat and cool slightly. Stir in chocolate-flavor liqueur and strain into sauceboat.

To serve, unmold desserts onto plates at least 30 minutes before serving to soften slightly. Fill a pie plate with hot water. Run a knife around the edge of each mold and dip into the hot water for 5 to 7 seconds. Dry bottom of mold; quickly cover dessert with a plate. Invert mold onto plate giving a firm shake; carefully remove mold.

Spoon a little of each sauce around each heart-shaped Bavarian cream. Garnish with grated chocolate and decorate with fresh mint.

FRENCH CHOCOLATE POTS DE CRÈME

8 SERVINGS

This classic French-style dessert of dark, creamy chocolate custard is really an upscale version of the classic American chocolate pudding, only richer. Use the darkest chocolate you can find.

2 cups milk
½ cup sugar
8 squares (8 oz.) bittersweet chocolate, chopped
1 tbsp. vanilla extract
2 tbsp. brandy or other liqueur
7 egg yolks
whipped cream, chopped pistachios and Chocolate Leaves (see Decorating with Chocolate) for garnish

Preheat oven to 325°F.

In a saucepan over medium heat, bring milk and sugar to a boil. Add chocolate all at once, stirring frequently until melted and smooth. Stir in vanilla and brandy.

In a bowl, beat egg yolks lightly. Slowly beat in chocolate mixture until well blended. Strain custard into an 8-cup measuring jug or large pitcher.

Place eight ½-cup *pots de crème* cups, custard cups or ramekins into a shallow roasting pan. Pour an equal amount of custard into each cup. Pour enough hot water into the pan to come about halfway up side of cups.

Bake 30 to 35 minutes, until custard is just set. Shake pan slightly; center of each custard should jiggle. Or, insert knife into side of 1 custard and knife should come out clean. Remove pan from oven and remove cups from pan to heat-proof surface to cool completely.

Place cooled custards on a cookie sheet and cover with plastic wrap. Refrigerate until well chilled. (The custards can be stored 2 to 3 days in the refrigerator.)

To serve, garnish the top of each custard with a dollop or rosette of whipped cream. Sprinkle each with chopped pistachios and a chocolate leaf.

FRENCH CHOCOLATE POTS DE CRÈME ►

CHOCOLATE-GLAZED CHOCOLATE ZUCCOTTO

8 TO 10 SERVINGS

This Florentine dessert was traditionally made in a pumpkin-shaped mold; zuccotto means "little pumpkin," but it is easily done in a mixing bowl.

1 chocolate roulade sponge (p.14)
½ cup almond-flavor liqueur
1 lb. ricotta cheese or 1 17½-oz. container mascarpone cheese
½ cup sugar
2 cups whipping cream
1 tbsp. vanilla extract
6 squares (6 oz.) bittersweet or semisweet chocolate, melted
2 tbsp. slivered almonds, toasted and chopped
grated zest of 1 orange plus 2 tbsp. juice
4 Amaretti cookies, broken into small pieces
⅓ cup candied fruit, chopped

CHOCOLATE GLAZE

4 tbsp. butter
3 tbsp. light corn syrup
4 squares (4 oz.) semisweet chocolate, chopped
extra grated orange zest for garnish

Prepare chocolate roulade sponge as on page 14. Line a 2½-qt. glass bowl with plastic wrap, allowing enough wrap to fold over bottom when dessert is finished. Cut cake in half lengthwise. Cut each strip into triangle-shaped pieces. Sprinkle cake pieces with 3 tbsp. almond-flavor liqueur and line bowl with cake pieces leaving no open spaces, pressing cake firmly against side of bowl. Reserve remaining cake pieces to make bottom.

If using ricotta cheese, press cheese through a strainer into large bowl. (This is not necessary for mascarpone cheese.) With a hand-held electric mixer, beat cheese and sugar until smooth.

In another bowl, beat whipping cream with vanilla until soft peaks form. Fold a spoonful of cream into cheese mixture to lighten, then fold in remaining cream. Divide mixture in half. Into half, fold melted chocolate and almonds; set aside. Into second half of cheese mixture, fold in orange zest and juice, remaining almond-flavor liqueur, Amaretti cookies and candied fruits.

Spoon the cheese-Amaretti mixture into the cake-lined bowl, spreading it to form an even layer all around bowl. Spoon the chocolate mixture into the center and smooth top. Cover top with the remaining cake pieces and fold over excess plastic wrap, pressing down lightly to create a flat bottom. Refrigerate 6 to 8 hours or overnight, until very firm.

Prepare glaze. In a saucepan over medium heat, melt butter, corn syrup and chocolate, stirring frequently until smooth. Cool slightly until mixture is thickened but still pourable.

Peel back plastic wrap from top of zuccotto and unmold onto a serving plate; remove plastic wrap. Pour over glaze, using a metal spatula to spread glaze evenly and scraping excess off dish. Clean plate. Refrigerate 5 minutes, until chocolate is set. Cut strips of waxed paper into triangles and place over dessert about 1½ in. apart. Dust with cocoa or confectioners' sugar. Garnish top with orange zest. Refrigerate until ready to serve.

Frozen Desserts

FROZEN PEANUT BUTTER-FUDGE TORTE

10–12 SERVINGS

Use store-bought ice cream to make this welcome summertime cooler. The combination of chocolate ice cream, peanut butter and fudge is a well-loved favorite.

CRUMB CRUST

8 oz. chocolate wafers (24–26)
½ cup dry-roasted peanuts, finely chopped and toasted
¼ cup (½ stick) unsalted butter, melted

FUDGE FILLING

½ cup heavy cream
3 tbsp. light corn syrup
5 squares (5 oz.) semisweet chocolate, chopped
1 tbsp. vanilla extract

ICE CREAM LAYER

3 pts. good-quality chocolate ice cream
¾ cup dry-roasted peanuts, chopped and toasted
1½ cups smooth peanut butter
¾ cup honey
1 cup whipping cream
¼ cup sugar
2 tsp. vanilla extract
chocolate-covered peanuts for garnish

Prepare crust. In a food processor, process chocolate wafer and peanuts until fine crumbs form. Pour in melted butter and process just until blended. Pat onto bottom and side of 9-in. springform pan.

Prepare filling. In a saucepan over medium heat, bring cream and corn syrup to a boil. Remove from the heat and add chocolate all at once, stirring until melted and smooth. Stir in vanilla. Set aside, stirring occasionally until slightly cooled. Pour into prepared pan. Cool completely while preparing ice-cream mixture.

Soften the ice cream 15 to 20 minutes at room temperature or until spreadable. In a bowl, combine nuts, peanut butter and honey until well blended. Add softened ice cream scoop by scoop and, using hand-held mixer on low speed, beat ice cream into the peanut-butter mixture just until mixed; do not let ice cream melt completely.

Pour ice-cream mixture into fudge-lined pan. Cover and freeze 4 to 6 hours or overnight until very firm.

Remove dessert from freezer and leave to soften 5 minutes at room temperature. Run a knife around edge of pan and remove side of pan.

With hand-held mixer, beat cream, sugar and vanilla just until stiff peaks form. Spoon cream into medium pastry bag fitted with medium star tip and pipe cream in attractive design on top of torte. Decorate with chocolate-covered peanuts.

SWEET SUCCESS

Torte can be prepared in 9- or 10-in. deep pie plate which does not require unmolding, but a springform pan gives a straight side which looks attractive when side is removed.

WHITE CHOCOLATE-RASPBERRY RIPPLE ICE CREAM

MAKES ABOUT 1 QUART

This sweet, creamy white chocolate ice cream is perfectly balanced by the slight tartness of the raspberry swirl. Serve with the left over Raspberry Ripple Sauce.

1 cup milk
2 cups whipping cream
7 egg yolks
2 tbsp. sugar
8 oz. fine-quality white chocolate, chopped

RASPBERRY RIPPLE SAUCE
1 10-oz. package frozen raspberries in light syrup
2 tsp. light corn syrup
1 tbsp. lemon juice
1 tbsp. cornstarch, diluted in 1 tbsp. water

Prepare sauce. Into a saucepan press raspberries and their syrup through a strainer. Add corn syrup, lemon juice and dissolved cornstarch. Bring to a boil, stirring frequently, then simmer 2 to 3 minutes, until sauce is thickened and syrupy. Pour into a bowl and cool to room temperature. Refrigerate sauce while preparing ice cream.

In a saucepan, bring milk and 1 cup cream to a boil. In a bowl with hand-held mixer, beat egg yolks and sugar until thick and creamy, 2 to 3 minutes. Gradually pour hot milk over yolks, then return mixture to saucepan.

Cook over medium heat until custard thickens and lightly coats the back of a wooden spoon, stirring constantly; do not let boil or custard will curdle.

Remove pan from heat and stir in chocolate until melted and smooth. Pour remaining 1 cup cold cream into a large bowl. Strain custard into bowl with cream. Blend well and cool to room temperature. Refrigerate until cold. Transfer custard to an ice-cream maker and freeze according to manufacturers' directions.

When mixture is frozen but still soft, transfer one-third of the ice cream to a bowl. Spoon over some of the raspberry ripple sauce in concentric circles. Cover with another third of the ice cream and then more raspberry sauce. Cover with the remaining ice cream and a little more raspberry sauce. With a knife or spoon, lightly marble raspberry sauce into the ice cream. Cover and freeze.

Leave ice cream to soften 20 to 30 minutes in the refrigerator before serving. Scoop into bowl and drizzle over some of the remaining raspberry sauce.

SWEET SUCCESS

Freeze ice cream in a soufflé dish or other attractive bowl rather than in a plastic container so it can be served directly at the table.

EASY FROZEN CHOCOLATE-MINT SOUFFLÉ

8 SERVINGS

This is a delicious dessert, rich yet light textured. The chocolate is flavored with a mint liqueur. Make sure you have a tall enough space in the freezer.

9 squares (9 oz.) bittersweet chocolate, broken into pieces
2 cups heavy cream
4 eggs, separated
3–4 tbsp. mint-flavor liqueur or 1 tbsp. mint-flavor extract
1/4 tsp. cream of tartar
1/4 cup sugar
grated chocolate for garnish

CHOCOLATE-DIPPED MINT LEAVES

20–24 fresh mint leaves
4 squares (4 oz.) semisweet or bittersweet chocolate, chopped

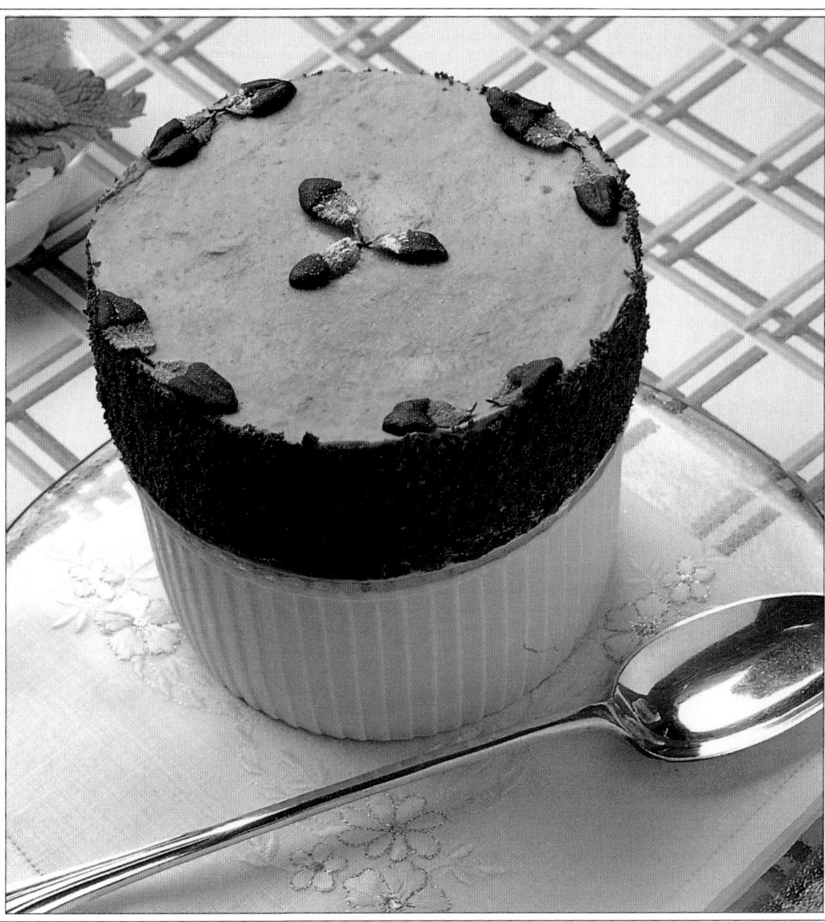

Prepare chocolate-dipped leaves. Rinse mint leaves in cold water and pat dry with paper towels. Line a cookie sheet with waxed paper.

In the top of a double boiler over low heat, melt chocolate, stirring frequently until smooth. Leave to cool to just below body temperature. Holding stem end, dip each mint leaf about halfway into chocolate, coating both sides, leaving excess chocolate to drip into bowl. Place coated leaves on cookie sheet and refrigerate; these leaves can be prepared 1 to 2 days ahead and refrigerated.

Prepare collar for soufflé dish. Cut a piece of waxed paper or foil long enough to encircle the dish, allowing a 2-in. overlap. Fold paper or foil in half lengthwise and wrap around dish so collar extends about 3 in. above side of dish. Secure paper or foil with tape or kitchen string. Lightly oil the paper collar; set dish aside.

Place chocolate into a food processor fitted with the metal blade or a blender.

In a saucepan, bring cream to a boil. With food processor or blender running, slowly pour cream over chocolate. Continue processing or blending until smooth, scraping the side of the container once.

With the machine still running, add the egg yolks, 1 at a time, processing well after each addition until well blended; chocolate mixture will be thick and creamy. Scrape into a bowl and stir in liqueur. Cool to room temperature; chocolate mixture will thicken further.

With electric mixer, beat egg whites and cream of tartar just until stiff peaks form. Add sugar, 2 tbsp. at a time, and continue beating just until whites are stiff and glossy; do not overbeat.

Stir 1 large spoonful of whites into chocolate mixture to lighten, then gently fold in remaining whites. Pour into the dish and freeze overnight. (Soufflé can be prepared 2 to 3 days ahead.)

To serve, remove tape or string from side of dish and, using a knife as a guide, carefully unwrap paper from dish and soufflé. Press grated chocolate onto side of soufflé and top with a few chocolate-coated mint leaves. Serve remaining leaves with each portion of soufflé.

SWEET SUCCESS

To ensure a "well-risen" soufflé, choose a tall, narrow soufflé dish not more than 5 or 6 ins. in diameter or soufflé mixture will not reach above edge of dish.

CHOCOLATE FROZEN YOGURT

MAKES 1 1/4 QUARTS

This dark, chocolate frozen yogurt is so creamy and delicious it's hard to believe it is so easy to make. Not only that – it is a dieter's answer to prayers – low fat!

1 quart plain lowfat yogurt
1⅓ cups sugar
⅔ cup unsweetened cocoa powder
1 tbsp. skim-milk powder, dissolved in 1–2 tbsp. milk or water

In a bowl with a wire whisk, mix together yogurt, sugar, cocoa and dissolved skim-milk powder until smooth and well blended and sugar is dissolved. Refrigerate 1 hour, until cold.

Transfer yogurt mixture to an ice-cream maker and freeze according to manufacturers directions; this mixture will not freeze as hard as ice cream. Transfer to a freezerproof serving bowl or container and freeze 3 to 4 hours, until firm. (Frozen yogurt can be stored in the freezer 2 to 3 weeks in a freezer-proof container).

VARIATION

For mocha frozen yogurt, use coffee-flavor low fat yogurt and add 1 tbsp. instant espresso or coffee powder, or experiment with other flavors.

RICH CHOCOLATE ICE CREAM

MAKES 1 1/4 QUARTS

This is a rich, smooth chocolaty ice cream, delicious on its own or as the basis for many variations.

8 squares (8 oz.) bittersweet chocolate, chopped
2 cups half-and-half or milk
3 egg yolks
1/4 cup sugar
1 1/2 cups heavy cream
1 tbsp. vanilla extract

In a saucepan over low heat, melt chocolate with 1/2 cup half-and-half, stirring frequently until smooth. Remove from heat.

In a saucepan over medium heat, bring remaining half-and-half to a boil. In a bowl with hand-held mixer, beat egg yolks and sugar until thick and creamy, 2 to 3 minutes. Gradually pour hot milk over yolks, beating constantly, then return mixture to saucepan.

Cook over medium heat until custard thickens and lightly coats the back of a wooden spoon, stirring constantly; do not let mixture boil or custard will curdle. Immediately pour melted chocolate over, stirring constantly until well blended.

Pour cold cream into a bowl and strain custard into bowl with cream. Blend well and cool to room temperature. Refrigerate until cold.

Transfer custard to an ice-cream maker and freeze according to manufacturers' directions. Leave to soften 15 to 20 minutes before serving.

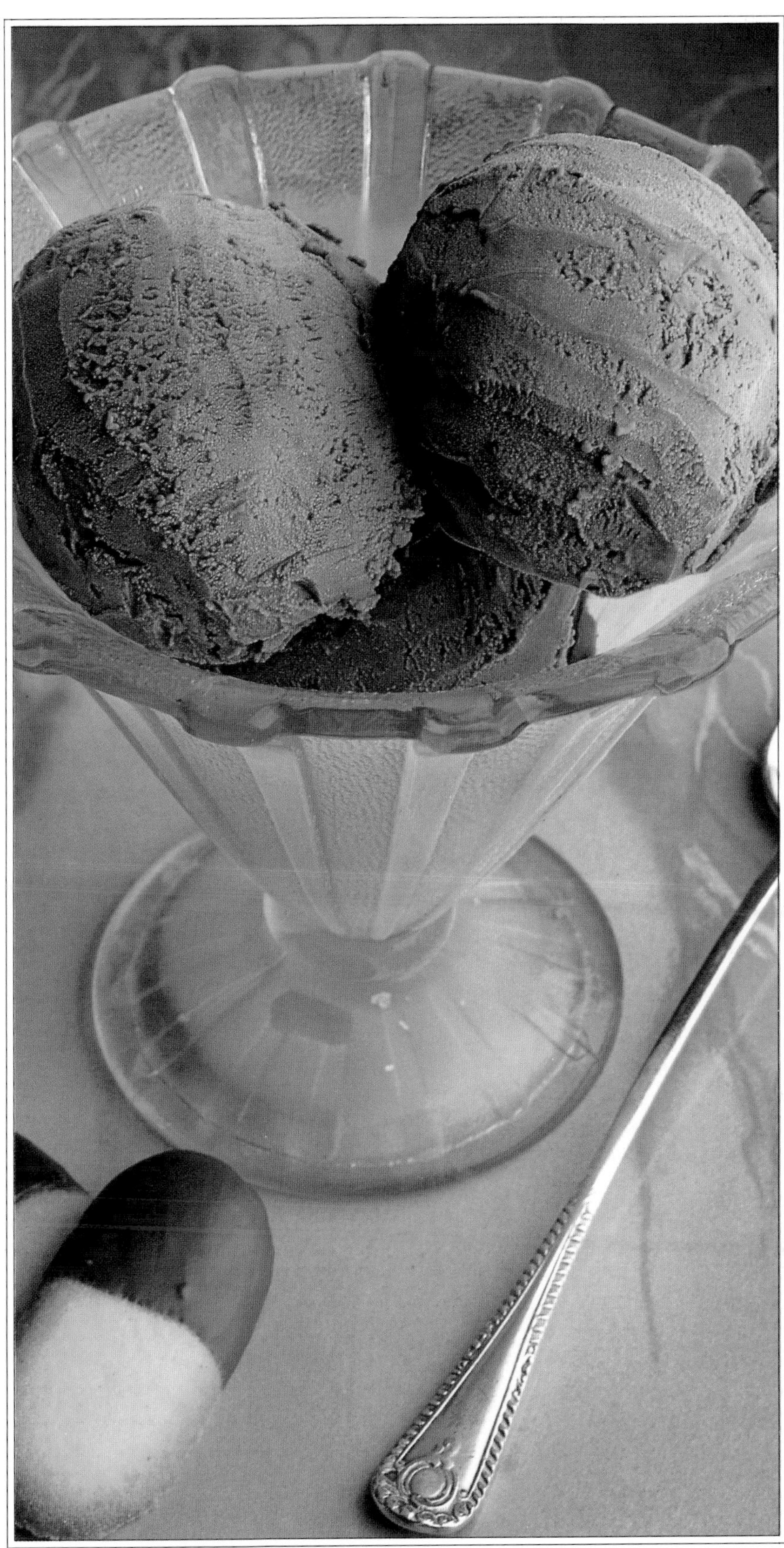

VARIATIONS

White, Dark, or Milk Chocolate Chunk – ***Stir 8 oz. fine-quality white, dark, or milk chocolate, chopped, into ice cream when removing from ice cream machine.***

Mocha Ice Cream – ***Prepare ice cream as directed but adding 2 tbsp. instant coffee or espresso powder, dissolved in 2 tbsp. water to melted chocolate before adding custard.***

MILK CHOCOLATE ICE MILK

MAKES 1 ¼ QUARTS

This is the easiest "ice cream" ever. The high milk content in milk chocolate gives the ice milk a very creamy texture without added eggs or cream.

16 ounces (1 lb.) fine-quality milk chocolate, chopped
1 cup half-and-half
2 cups milk (not skim or 2% fat)
whipped cream for garnish

In a saucepan over low heat, melt chocolate with half-and-half, stirring frequently until smooth. Gradually stir in milk, beating until smooth and well-blended. Cook over low heat 5 to 7 minutes. Strain into a large bowl and cool to room temperature, stirring occasionally. Cover and refrigerate 6 to 8 hours or overnight.

If mixture has separated slightly, stir well. Transfer to an ice-cream maker and freeze according to manufacturers' directions. Leave to soften 10 to 15 minutes at room temperature before serving. Serve garnished with whipped cream or chocolate sauce.

VARIATION

Mocha-Milk Chocolate Ice Milk – ***Prepare as above but add 2 tbsp. instant coffee or espresso powder dissolved in 2 tbsp. water to half-and-half or milk.***

CHOCOLATE-PECAN PARFAIT

10 SERVINGS

A parfait is a dessert mixture similar to a frozen mousse. This delicious chocolate mixture contains a surprise filling of pecan praline and chunks of milk chocolate.

2 cups heavy cream
9 squares (9 oz.) bittersweet or semisweet chocolate, chopped
3 egg yolks
2 tbsp. almond- or hazelnut-flavor liqueur
2 oz. fine-quality milk chocolate, chopped into small pieces

PECAN PRALINE

vegetable oil for cookie sheet
1 cup pecan halves
1 cup sugar
$\frac{1}{4}$ cup water
Chocolate Curls (see Decorating with Chocolate) for garnish

Prepare praline. Preheat oven to 350°F. Oil a cookie sheet and set aside. Spread pecan halves onto another cookie sheet and bake 10 to 12 minutes, until pecans are well toasted.

In a saucepan over medium heat, heat sugar and water until the sugar dissolves, swirling the pan occasionally. Leave sugar to come to a boil and continue boiling until sugar turns a golden caramel color. Stir in toasted pecans, then pour mixture onto the oiled cookie sheet to cool and harden. Do not touch as caramel can stick and cause serious burns.

Leave praline to cool to room temperature. When hard, place in a deep bowl and crush with the end of a rolling pin or place in a heavy plastic bag and crush with a rolling pin. Set aside.

Line an 8- × 4-in. loaf pan with plastic wrap, allowing enough wrap to fold over bottom when parfait is finished.

In a saucepan over medium heat, bring 1 cup cream to a boil. Remove from the heat and add the chocolate all at once, stirring until melted and smooth. Add egg yolks, 1 at a time, beating well after each addition. Strain into a bowl and stir in the liqueur. Set aside to cool and thicken.

In a bowl, beat remaining cream until soft peaks form; do not overbeat or cream will not blend into the chocolate mixture. Stir 1 spoonful cream into chocolate mixture to lighten, then fold in remaining cream just until blended.

Spoon one-third of the chocolate mixture into bottom of loaf pan, spreading evenly. Sprinkle one-quarter of the praline over and then one half of the milk chocolate. Spoon another third of the chocolate mixture over, spreading to cover praline and chocolate. Sprinkle another quarter of the praline mixture and remaining milk chocolate over; spread with remaining chocolate mixture, smoothing top evenly. Fold over excess plastic wrap to cover parfait. Freeze 6 to 8 hours or overnight.

To serve, peel back plastic wrap from the top of the parfait. Invert onto serving plate and remove plastic wrap. Press remaining crushed praline onto sides of parfait and sprinkle a little on the top. Garnish top with chocolate curls. Leave parfait to soften about 30 minutes in the refrigerator before cutting into thin slices.

CHOCOLATE-STRAWBERRY FROZEN DAQUOISE

10 SERVINGS

Meringue freezes beautifully, so this is an ideal dessert to make ahead and store in the freezer. Leave the daquoise to soften about 30 minutes in the refrigerator before serving.

1¼ cups sugar
2 tbsp. unsweetened cocoa powder, sifted
5 egg whites
¼ tsp. cream of tartar
1 pt. good-quality chocolate ice cream
1 pt. good-quality strawberry ice cream
1 pt. fresh strawberries
2 cups whipping cream
¼ cup sugar
2 tbsp. raspberry-flavor liqueur

STRAWBERRY SAUCE
2 10-oz. packages frozen strawberries in syrup, drained
1 tbsp. lemon juice
10 Chocolate-dipped Strawberries (p105) for garnish

CHOCOLATE-STRAWBERRY FROZEN DAQUOISE ►

Preheat oven to 275°F. Line 1 large and 1 small cookie sheet with nonstick parchment paper or foil. Using an 8-in. cake pan or plate as a guide, mark 2 circles on the large cookie sheet and 1 circle on the small cookie sheet.

In a bowl, mix together ¼ cup sugar and cocoa powder. Set aside.

With electric mixer, beat egg whites and cream of tartar until stiff peaks form. Gradually sprinkle remaining sugar over, a little at a time, beating well after each addition, until whites are stiff and glossy. Gently fold in cocoa-sugar mixture just until blended.

Spoon one-third of the meringue mixture inside each marked circle on cookie sheets. Spread each meringue out evenly to an 8-in. circle, smoothing tops and edges.

Bake meringues 1¼ hours, until crisp and dry. Remove to wire racks to cool 10 minutes on cookie sheets. Then remove meringues from parchment paper or foil to cool completely; meringues can be stored in an airtight container if not using at once.

Place meringue layers on a freezerproof serving plate and freeze for 20 minutes; this makes them firmer and easier to handle while spreading ice cream. Meanwhile, remove chocolate and strawberry ice creams from freezer to soften 15 to 20 minutes at room temperature.

Remove meringue layers and serving plate from freezer. Place 1 meringue layer on the plate and spread with chocolate ice cream to within ½-in. of edge. Cover with a second meringue layer and spread with strawberry ice cream to within ½ in. of edge. Top with third meringue layer, pressing layers gently together. Return to freezer 5 to 6 hours or overnight.

In a bowl with hand-held mixer, beat cream, sugar and raspberry liqueur until soft peaks form. Remove meringue layers from the freezer and spread top and side with cream in a swirling or decorative pattern. Freeze until ready to serve if not using at once.

For the sauce, process strawberries in a food processor with metal blade attached, until well blended. Press purée through a strainer into a bowl. Stir in lemon juice and if sauce is too thick, thin with a little water.

To serve, slice fresh strawberries lengthwise and decorate top of daquoise. Serve each slice of daquoise with some strawberry sauce and a chocolate-dipped strawberry.

CHOCOLATE-ORANGE SHERBET

MAKES 3 PINTS

A sherbet can be made with a fruit purée and a sugar syrup or with milk. Milk gives this dark sherbet a rich, velvety texture.

4 squares (4 oz.) bittersweet chocolate, chopped
2 cups milk
1¼ cups sugar
¾ cup unsweetened cocoa powder
1 6-oz. container frozen orange juice concentrate, thawed

In a saucepan over low heat, melt chocolate with ½ cup milk, stirring frequently until smooth. Set aside to cool.

In a bowl, combine sugar and cocoa powder. Make a well in center of the mixture and, with a wire whisk, gradually stir in remaining milk, bringing in more and more of the cocoa mixture until all the cocoa-milk mixture is smooth. Beat in orange-juice concentrate and orange zest.

Slowly beat cocoa-milk into melted chocolate until well blended. Refrigerate at least 1 hour, until cold.

Transfer mixture to an ice-cream maker and freeze according to manufacturers' directions; this mixture will not freeze as hard as ice cream. Transfer to a serving bowl or container and freeze 3 to 4 hours, until firm. (Sherbet can be stored in the freezer 2 to 3 weeks in a freezerproof container).

FROZEN CHOCOLATE-CHERRY MOUSSE RING

8 SERVINGS

This simple chocolate mousse is served with a fresh cherry sauce and garnished with Chocolate-dipped Cherries. The same sauce is delicious with Rich Chocolate Ice Cream.

8 squares (8 oz.) bittersweet or semisweet chocolate, chopped
2 tbsp. cherry-flavor liqueur
2 tbsp. water
4 eggs, separated
¼ tsp. cream of tartar
¼ cup sugar
¾ cup whipping cream

POACHED CHERRIES
2 lbs. fresh sweet cherries
1 orange
½ cup sugar
2 cups sugar
¼ cup seedless raspberry preserves or red currant jelly
1 tbsp. cornstarch, dissolved in 1 tbsp. cold water
1 cup whipping cream
1 tbsp. sugar
1 tbsp. cherry-flavor liqueur
fresh mint leaves and Chocolate-dipped Cherries (see Double Chocolate-Dipped Fruit in Candies chapter)

Lightly oil a 5-cup freezerproof ring or other mold. In a saucepan over low heat, melt chocolate with cherry-flavor liqueur and water, stirring frequently until smooth. Remove from heat and beat in egg yolks, 1 at a time, beating well after each addition.

With electric mixer, beat whites and cream of tartar until soft peaks form. Gradually add sugar, 1 tbsp. at a time, beating well after each addition, until white are stiff and glossy but not dry. Fold a spoonful of whites into chocolate mixture to lighten, then fold in remaining chocolate.

With hand-held electric mixer, beat cream just until soft peaks form. Fold into chocolate mixture, then pour mousse into the prepared mold. Cover mold with plastic wrap and freeze 6 to 8 hours or overnight. (Mousse can be stored covered in the freezer for 1 to 2 days.)

Prepare cherries. Remove stems and using a cherry pitter or small knife, remove pits. Using a swivel-bladed vegetable peeler, remove zest from orange and squeeze juice. Place in a saucepan with sugar and water. Bring to a boil, then reduce heat. Add cherries to poaching liquid and simmer 7 to 10 minutes, until tender. Remove from heat and leave cherries in poaching liquid 3 to 4 hours.

Using a slotted spoon, remove cherries from liquid to a bowl. Add raspberry preserves and dissolved cornstarch to syrup and bring to a boil, then reduce heat and simmer 1 to 2 minutes until syrup is thickened and coats the back of a spoon. Strain over cherries and cool to room temperature. Refrigerate 4 to 6 hours or overnight until completely chilled.

To unmold mousse, run a thin-bladed knife around outer and inner edges of mold. Dip mold into warm water to come about halfway up side of mold 5 seconds. Dry bottom of mold; quickly cover with serving plate. Invert mold onto plate, giving a firm shake; remove mold. Smooth surface with metal spatula and return to freezer for 5 minutes to chill surface.

To serve, beat cream, sugar and cherry-flavor liqueur until soft peaks form. Spoon one-quarter of cream into a small pastry bag fitted with a medium star tip and pipe a decorative border around edge of mold; spoon remaining cream into center of mold. Decorate outer edge with mint leaves and chocolate-dipped cherries and serve cherries in their sauce separately.

ROCKY ROAD ICE CREAM PIE WITH ROCKY ROAD SAUCE

10 SERVINGS

The combination of chocolate marshmallows and pecans is a classic one. This pie uses a soft-cocoa fudge between the ice cream layers and a chocolaty, marshmallow sauce over it!

CRUMB CRUST

8 oz. chocolate wafers (24–26) (makes about 1½ cups crumbs)
½ cup pecans, chopped and toasted
¼ cup (½ stick) unsalted butter, melted

COCOA FUDGE

¾ cup sugar
2 tbsp. unsweetened cocoa powder
1 tbsp. light corn syrup
½ cup whipping cream
1 tbsp. butter
2 pts. good-quality store-bought Rocky Road or chocolate ice cream
2 cups mini-marshmallows
1 cup whipping cream
¾ cup sugar
1 tsp. vanilla extract

ROCKY ROAD SAUCE

2 squares (2 oz.) bittersweet or semisweet chocolate, chopped
1 cup mini-marshmallows
⅓ cup whipping cream
⅓ cup honey
Chocolate-dipped Pecan Halves (p9) ***or*** **chopped pecans for garnish**

Preheat oven to 400°F. In a food processor, process chocolate wafers and pecans until fine crumbs form. Pour in melted butter and process just until blended. Press onto bottom and side of 9-in. pie plate.

Bake piecrust 6 to 8 minutes, until set. Cool on wire rack completely. Freeze piecrust 20 minutes while preparing ice cream.

Soften 1 pt. ice cream 15 to 20 minutes at room temperature. Spread ice cream onto bottom of frozen crust, smoothing surface evenly. Return to freezer until completely firm.

In a saucepan over medium heat, bring sugar, cocoa, corn syrup, cream and butter to a boil, stirring constantly until smooth. Remove from heat.

Remove pie plate from freezer and while cocoa fudge is still warm, pour over ice cream layer. Immediately sprinkle mini-marshmallows over, pressing them into the fudge layer with the back of a spoon, so warm fudge melts them slightly. Return pie to freezer, 25 to 30 minutes.

Soften remaining ice cream 20 minutes at room temperature. Remove pie from freezer and spread ice cream over fudge layer, spreading ice cream to edge of crust and covering completely. Return pie to freezer and freeze 4 to 6 hours or overnight.

With hand-held electric mixer, beat cream, sugar and vanilla just until stiff peaks form. Spread cream over pie to edge of crust in a swirling pattern and garnish with chocolate-dipped pecans or sprinkle with chopped pecans.

Leave pie to soften 30 minutes in refrigerator or 20 minutes at room temperature before serving. (Pie can be prepared up to 1 week ahead and stored in freezer.)

Prepare sauce. In a heavy-bottomed saucepan over low heat, melt chocolate and marshmallows with cream and honey, stirring frequently until smooth and well blended. Pour into sauceboat and serve warm over slices of ice cream pie.

DOUBLE CHOCOLATE RUM-RAISIN BOMBE

10 SERVINGS

This rich, raisin-studded chocolate ice cream dessert contains a soft center of white chocolate mousse. Garnish with Chocolate-dipped Prunes if you like.

CHOCOLATE RUM-RAISIN ICE CREAM

½ cup dark or golden raisins
¼ cup plus 1 tbsp. light rum
5 squares (5 oz.) white chocolate, chopped
1 square (1 oz.) unsweetened chocolate, chopped
1⅓ cups milk
3 egg yolks
2 tbsp. sugar
¼ cup honey
1 cup whipping cream

WHITE CHOCOLATE MOUSSE

½ cup golden raisins
3 tbsp light rum
1 cup whipping cream
5 oz. fine-quality white chocolate, chopped
2 egg whites
¼ tsp. cream of tartar
¼ cup sugar
2 tbsp. sugar
1 tbsp. unsweetened cocoa powder
1 tbsp. light rum
½ cup whipping cream
10 Chocolate-dipped Prunes (see recipe in Candies chapter)

In a bowl, mix raisins and ¼ cup rum. Leave to stand at least 2 hours, stirring occasionally.

In a saucepan over low heat, melt both chocolates with ⅓ cup milk, stirring frequently until smooth. Set aside.

In another saucepan, bring remaining 1 cup milk to a boil. In a bowl with hand-held mixer, beat egg yolks with the sugar and honey until pale and thick, about 2 minutes. Pour about 1 cup hot milk over the yolks and return the mixture to the pan.

Cook egg-and-milk custard over low heat until mixture thickens and lightly coats the back of a spoon, stirring constantly, 5 to 7 minutes. Stir hot custard into the melted chocolate mixture until well blended.

Place the cold cream in a large bowl and strain hot chocolate custard mixture over – beat together until well blended; cold cream stops the custard cooking. Stir in remaining 1 tbsp. rum and leave to cool, stirring occasionally. Refrigerate 2 to 3 hours until well chilled.

Transfer custard to an ice-cream maker and freeze according to manufacturers' directions. Remove to a large bowl and stir in rum-soaked raisins, then freeze until firm, at least 2 hours.

Chill a 1½ qt. ice cream bombe mold or freezerproof glass mixing bowl in the freezer. Remove ice cream from freezer to soften at room temperature, about 15 minutes. When bowl is chilled and ice cream softened, spread ice cream in an even layer on base and up side of chilled mold or bowl using the back of a spoon to smooth. Return to freezer.

Prepare mousse. In a small bowl, mix raisins and ¼ cup rum. Leave to stand at least 2 hours, stirring occasionally.

In a saucepan over low heat, bring ¼ cup cream to a boil. Remove from heat and stir in chocolate all at once until melted and smooth. Stir in remaining 1 tbsp. rum and rum-soaked raisins and set aside to cool.

With electric mixer, beat egg whites and cream of tartar until stiff peaks form. Sprinkle sugar over, 1 tbsp. at a time, beating well after each addition, until whites are stiff and glossy. Stir 1 spoonful of whites into melted chocolate mixture to lighten, then fold in remaining whites.

In another bowl with hand-held electric mixer, beat remaining whipping cream until soft peaks form. Fold in mousse mixture, then fold in soaked raisins.

Remove ice cream-lined bombe or bowl from freezer and fill with the white chocolate mousse. Cover and freeze 6 to 8 hours or overnight. (Bombe can be prepared 1 week ahead and stored in freezer.)

Remove bombe from freezer and uncover. Dip a thin-bladed knife into hot water and dry. Quickly run knife around side of mold to loosen ice cream. Dip mold or bowl into warm water, about halfway up side of mold, about 5 seconds. Dry mold and run knife or spatula around side again until bombe is released. Set a serving plate over mold and invert mold onto plate with a firm shake. Smooth surface and return to freezer to set surface.

Stir together sugar and cocoa, making a well in center. Slowly stir in cream until sugar and cocoa are well dissolved. Add the rum and, with a hand-held mixer, beat cream just until stiff peaks form; do not overbeat.

Spoon cocoa-flavored cream into small pastry bag fitted with a medium star tip. Pipe a swirl of cream around edge of mold and decorate with the Chocolate-dipped Prunes. If you like, pipe a few rosettes around top edge or 1 rosette in center. Leave bombe to soften 10 to 15 minutes at room temperature or 20 to 30 minutes in refrigerator.

Cadbury's
BOURNVILLE
COCOA
FOR
THE REAL
CADBURY
FLAVOUR

FROZEN CHOCOLATE-COATED BANANA POPS

6 SERVINGS

All children love banana and these chocolate-coated bananas on a stick are special favorites all year round. Cut and freeze extra bananas any time and they'll be ready for coating at a moments notice.

3 bananas, unbruised and fully ripe
8 squares (8 oz.) semisweet or bittersweet chocolate, chopped
3 tbsp. vegetable shortening
½ cup unsalted peanuts, chopped

Line a small cookie sheet with waxed paper. Peel bananas, being sure to remove all stringy fibers. Cut each in half crosswise, then insert a wooden pop-type stick 1½ ins. into cut-end of each banana half. Place on lined cookie-sheet and freeze 3 hours or overnight, until very firm.

In a saucepan, melt chocolate and vegetable shortening, stirring frequently until smooth. Pour into a tall mug or paper cup or other tall, narrow container. Leave chocolate to cool 10 to 15 minutes, until thickening slightly.

Spread peanuts onto a small flat plate or piece of waxed paper or foil. Hold 1 banana by the stick and dip into chocolate, tilting mug or cup and twisting banana until completely coated in chocolate. Quickly pull out banana and hold upright, then immediately roll in chopped nuts just until lightly coated.

Place on waxed paper-lined cookie sheet and place in freezer to harden. Continue with each pop and place each on prepared cookie sheet as soon as it is coated. Freeze at least 1 hour, until chocolate is completely hardened. (Pops can be stored covered in the freezer for 1 to 2 weeks – if they last that long!)

SWEET SUCCESS

Do not use metal sticks or small pointed wooden skewers as they could be harmful or cause injury to small children. Pop-style sticks are available in larger supermarkets or cook stores.

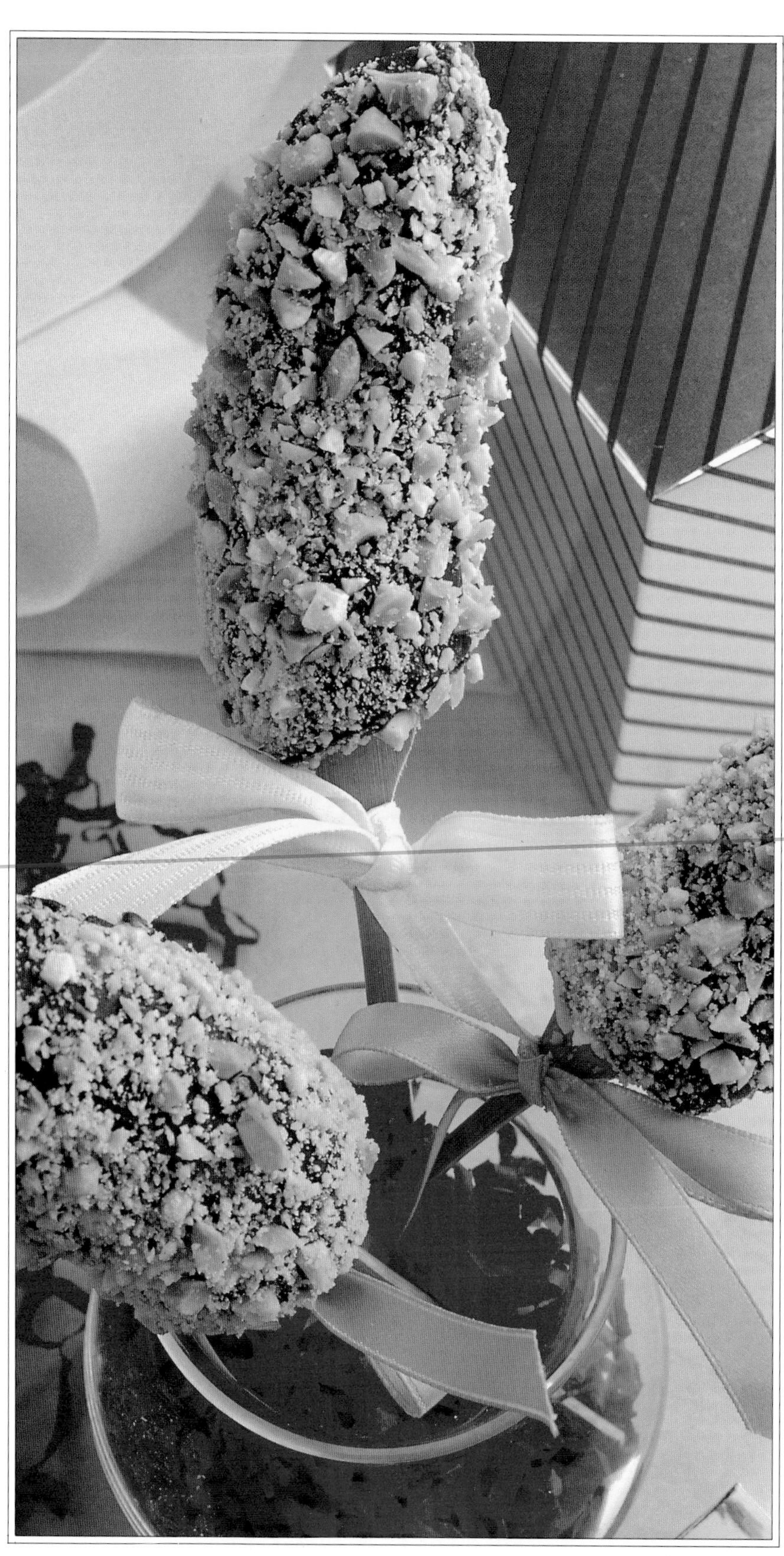

DOUBLE CHOCOLATE BROWNIE-BAKED ALASKA

8 TO 10 SERVINGS

This frozen dessert is an ideal party piece as it can be prepared well ahead and stored in the freezer until ready for baking. Use homemade or good-quality bought ice creams and any combination you like.

1 batch Rich Chocolate Ice Cream (p65) or 1 pt. good-quality chocolate ice cream
1 batch White Chocolate-Raspberry Ripple Ice Cream (p62) or 1 pt. good-quality vanilla ice cream
1 pt. good-quality raspberry sherbet
4 egg whites, at room temperature
¼ tsp. cream of tartar
1 cup sugar
2 tsp. vanilla extract

BROWNIE LAYER
½ cup (1 stick) unsalted butter, cut into pieces
2 squares (2 oz.) unsweetened chocolate, chopped
1 cup sugar
2 eggs
1 tsp. vanilla extract
½ cup all-purpose flour
½ cup pecans, chopped and toasted
fresh raspberries for garnish

Prepare brownie layer. Preheat oven to 350°F. Lightly grease and flour an 8-in. cake pan.

In a saucepan over low heat, melt butter and chocolate, stirring frequently until smooth. Remove from heat and stir in sugar, eggs and vanilla and beat just until blended. Stir in flour and pecans just until blended. Spoon into pan.

Bake 25 to 30 minutes, until a slight indentation remains on top when touched lightly with a fingertip. Remove to wire rack to cool to room temperature. Invert onto wire rack to cool completely. Wrap tightly in plastic wrap until ready to use.

Line a 6-to 8-cup freezerproof mixing bowl with a flat bottom and diameter of not more than 8 ins. with plastic wrap, allowing enough wrap to fold over bottom when dessert is finished.

Soften chocolate ice cream at room temperature 15 to 20 minutes or until it can be easily scooped. Spread the ice cream into an even 1-in. layer around the bowl to within ½ in. of top of bowl. Cover and freeze 15 to 20 minutes. Meanwhile, remove white chocolate ice cream from freezer to soften.

When white chocolate ice cream is soft enough to spread, remove chocolate ice cream-lined bowl from freezer. Spread white chocolate ice cream into an even layer against the chocolate layer, about 1 in. thick. Cover, then refreeze 15 to 20 minutes. Meanwhile, remove raspberry sherbet from freezer to soften.

Fill center of bowl with raspberry sherbet and smooth the surface evenly. Place the brownie layer onto the surface of the ice cream-filled bowl and press against the surface; trim to fit if necessary. Fold plastic wrap over top of bowl and return to freezer at least 6 hours or overnight.

Peel back plastic wrap from top of bowl. Invert bowl onto an ovenproof serving plate. Remove plastic wrap from ice cream and return plate to freezer.

Preheat oven to 500°F. With an electric mixer, beat whites and cream of tartar until stiff peaks form. Gradually add sugar, beating well after each addition, until peaks are stiff and glossy. Beat in vanilla.

Spread about 2 tbsp. meringue over top of dessert. Spoon remaining meringue into a large pastry bag fitted with a medium star tip and pipe vertical stripes, with edges touching, around side of molded dessert. Be sure all edges around side of dessert and bottom are well sealed. Pipe a pretty border around edge of flat top of the dessert, making an edge to contain garnish. (Dessert can be frozen at this stage up to 1 hour ahead if necessary.)

Bake 3 to 5 minutes, until meringue is golden and set. Fill top of meringue with fresh raspberries and serve with raspberry sauce.

SWEET SUCCESS

If using White Chocolate Raspberry-Ripple Ice Cream and Rich Chocolate Ice Cream, you will not need all the ice cream each recipe yields, but it is impractical to make these ice creams in smaller quantities. Store any left over ice cream in small, freezerproof containers.

Cookies and Brownies

CHOCOLATE CHUNK CHOCOLATE DROPS

CHOCOLATE "AMARETTI" COOKIES

BITTERSWEET FUDGE COOKIES

CHOCOLATE FEATHERED TUILES

CHOCOLATE-FILLED CIGARETTE COOKIES

CHOCOLATE-CHIP PECAN SHORTBREAD

CHOCOLATE CHIP-GINGER FLORENTINES

BRANDIED BROWNIE "TART"

CHOCOLATE VIENNESE COOKIES

CHOCOLATE CRACKLE TOPS

CHOCOLATE-HAZELNUT PINWHEELS

WHITE CHOCOLATE FRUIT N' NUT BARS

BLACK-AND-WHITE CHOCOLATE-MINT SANDWICH COOKIES

CHUNKY CHOCOLATE BROWNIES WITH FUDGE GLAZE

CHOCOLATE-PECAN MERINGUES

CHOCOLATE-COCONUT SARAH BERNHARDTS

COCOA BROWNIES WITH
MILK CHOCOLATE-WALNUT TOPPING

CREAM CHEESE-MARBLED BROWNIES

CHOCOLATE CHUNK CHOCOLATE DROPS

MAKES ABOUT 18

These are very big chocolate cookies which are filled with chunks of chocolate and nuts. They are thin and crisp near the edges but soft and fudgy inside.

6 squares (6 oz.) bittersweet or semisweet chocolate, chopped
½ cup (1 stick) unsalted butter, cut into pieces
2 eggs
½ cup sugar
¼ cup packed brown sugar
⅓ cup all-purpose flour
¼ cup cocoa powder
1 tsp. baking powder
2 tsp. vanilla extract
¼ tsp. salt
1 cup pecans, toasted and chopped
1 cup semisweet-chocolate chips
4 oz. fine-quality white chocolate, chopped into ¼-in. pieces
4 oz. fine-quality milk chocolate, chopped into ¼-in. pieces

Preheat oven to 325°F. Grease 2 large cookie sheets. In a medium saucepan over low heat, melt chocolate and butter, stirring frequently until smooth. Remove from heat to cool slightly.

With electric mixer, beat eggs and sugars until thick and pale, 2 to 3 minutes. Gradually pour in melted chocolate, beating until well blended. Beat in flour, cocoa powder, baking powder, vanilla and salt just until blended. Stir in nuts, chocolate chips and chocolate pieces.

Drop heaping tablespoonsful of dough, at least 4 ins. apart, flattening dough slightly, trying to keep about a 3 in. circle; you will only get 4 to 6 cookies on each sheet. Bake 10 to 12 minutes, until tops are cracked and shiny; do not overbake or they will break when removed from cookie sheet.

Remove cookies to wire rack to cool until firm, but not too crisp. Before they become too crisp, remove each cookie to wire rack to cool completely. Continue to bake in batches. Store cookies in an airtight container.

SWEET SUCCESS

If you need to use the same cookie sheets to bake in batches, cool by running back of cookie sheet under cold water and wiping surface with a paper towel before re-greasing.

CHOCOLATE "AMARETTI" COOKIES

ABOUT 2 DOZEN

These chocolate-almond meringue cookies are based on the popular Italian Amaretti cookie. They are easy to make and are the ideal accompaniment to espresso coffee.

1 cup blanched whole almonds
½ cup superfine sugar
1 tbsp. unsweetened cocoa powder
2 tbsp. confectioners' sugar
2 egg whites
⅛ tsp. cream of tartar
1 tsp. almond extract
confectioners' sugar for dusting

Preheat oven to 350°F. Place almonds on a small cookie sheet and bake 10 to 12 minutes, stirring occasionally, until golden brown. Remove from oven and cool to room temperature; reduce oven temperature to 325°F.

Line a large cookie sheet with non-stick parchment paper or foil.

In a food processor fitted with the metal blade, process almonds with ¼ cup sugar until almonds are finely ground, but not oily. Transfer to a bowl and sift in cocoa powder and confectioners' sugar; stir to blend. Set aside.

With electric mixer, beat egg whites and cream of tartar until soft peaks form. Sprinkle in remaining ¼ cup sugar, 1 tbsp. at a time, beating well after each addition, until whites are glossy and stiff. Beat in almond extract.

Sprinkle almond-sugar mixture over and gently fold into beaten whites just until blended. Spoon mixture into a large pastry bag fitted with a medium, plain ½-in. tip. Pipe 1½-in. circles about 1 in. apart onto prepared cookie sheet.

Bake 12 to 15 minutes, or until cookies appear crisp. Remove to wire rack to cool 10 minutes. With metal spatula, remove cookies to wire rack to cool completely. When cool, dust with confectioners' sugar and store in an air-tight container.

SWEET SUCCESS

As an alternative decoration, lightly press a few coffee-sugar crystals onto top of each cookie before baking.

BITTERSWEET FUDGE COOKIES

MAKES 36

These chocolaty drop cookies are easy to make, but the batter should be allowed to chill before handling. Firm on the outside, these cookies are dark and fudgy on the inside. Use the best-quality chocolate you can find.

6 squares (6 oz.) bittersweet chocolate, chopped
½ cup (1 stick) unsalted butter, at room temperature
½ cup sugar
2 eggs
1 tsp. vanilla extract
1½ cups all-purpose flour
½ tsp. salt
1 cup pecans, chopped and toasted
3 oz. fine-quality white chocolate, chopped into ¼-in. pieces
melted chocolate for garnish

In the top of a double boiler over low heat, melt chocolate, stirring frequently until smooth. Remove from heat.

With electric mixer, cream butter, sugar, eggs and vanilla until creamy and smooth, 2 to 3 minutes, scraping bowl occasionally. Slowly beat in the cooled chocolate until well blended.

Gradually stir in flour and salt, stirring just until blended. Stir in the pecans and chopped white chocolate. Cover bowl with plastic wrap and refrigerate 1 hour or until firm.

Meanwhile, preheat the oven to 375°F. Lightly grease 2 large cookie sheets. Drop dough by rounded teaspoonsful at least 2 ins. apart onto the prepared cookie sheets, flattening slightly; it may take 2 batches.

Bake 8 to 10 minutes, or just until surface feels slightly firm when touched with a fingertip. Remove cookie sheets to wire racks to cool 5 to 7 minutes. With a metal spatula, remove cookies to wire rack to cool completely. Repeat with remaining dough. When cool, drizzle chocolate over them using a spoon and store in airtight containers.

CHOCOLATE FEATHERED TUILES

MAKES 10–12

These wafer-thin cookies are called* tuiles *in French because they resemble the roof tiles used on houses. They are the perfect cookie to accompany ice creams, mousses and custard desserts. These have an added feather pattern which is fussy to make – but worth the effort!

1 egg white
¼ cup superfine sugar
2 tbsp. all-purpose flour, sifted
½ tsp. vanilla extract
2 tbsp. unsalted butter, melted
1 tsp. unsweetened cocoa powder

Preheat oven to 375°F. Generously grease 2 large cookie sheets; you will need to work in batches.

With hand-held mixer, beat egg white just until stiff. Gradually beat in sugar, 1 tablespoon at a time, beating well after each addition, until the whites are glossy and stiff.

Fold sifted flour and vanilla into the egg whites, then fold in butter. Gently spoon about 2 tbsp. batter into a small bowl and fold cocoa into the smaller amount of batter. Spoon the cocoa batter into a small pastry bag fitted with a small writing tip or a paper cone (see Decorating with Chocolate). Set aside.

Drop plain batter by rounded teaspoonsful, at least 3 ins. apart, onto prepared cookie sheets. Using the back of a spoon or metal spatula spread out batter to about 3 ins. in diameter.

Pipe 4 or 5 lines of cocoa-batter crosswise across each circle, then draw a skewer or toothpick lengthwise through lines in alternate directions to create a feather pattern.

Bake 4 to 5 minutes, until edges begin to turn brown and appear set. Using a metal spatula, immediately lift each tuile from the cookie sheet and place, top-side up, over a rolling pin to curl and set; cool completely. If tuiles begin to harden before you have them over the rolling pin, return to oven 15 to 20 seconds to soften enough to remove without breaking. Continue in batches until all batter is used. (Store up to 2 days in an airtight container.)

SWEET SUCCESS

For chocolate tuiles or tulips, add the cocoa to all the plain batter and omit feathering process. Drape plain cooked tuile over small juice glasses to create small tulip shapes to fill with ice cream, sherbet, mousse or custard desserts.

CHOCOLATE-FILLED CIGARETTE COOKIES

MAKES 10–12

These delicate, melt-in-the-mouth cookies use Chocolate Feathered Tuiles. Rolled into cigarette shapes, they are then filled with a creamy, rich chocolate ganache.

Chocolate Feathered Tuiles (p80)

CHOCOLATE GANACHE

6 squares (6 oz.) bittersweet or semisweet chocolate, chopped
½ cup heavy cream
2 tbsp. almond-flavor liqueur

Prepare ganache. In a medium saucepan over medium heat, bring cream to a boil. Add chocolate all at once, stirring until melted and smooth. Remove from heat and stir in almond-flavor liqueur. Cool 2 to 3 hours, until thickened to piping consistency.

Meanwhile, prepare tuile batter, but substitute almond extract for the vanilla and add the cocoa to all the plain batter.

Bake tuiles as on p80. Remove tuiles from cookie sheet and roll each around the handle of a wooden spoon or pencil. Press along edge to seal, then leave to set about 2 minutes. Continue shaping each cookie until all cookies are rolled into a cigarette shape. Cool as directed.

Spoon ganache into a medium pastry bag fitted with a small writing tip; be sure tip can fit into each "cigarette" cookie. Pipe some ganache into each cookie and set aside. Do not refrigerate or ganache will become too firm. Serve with ice cream or after-dinner coffee.

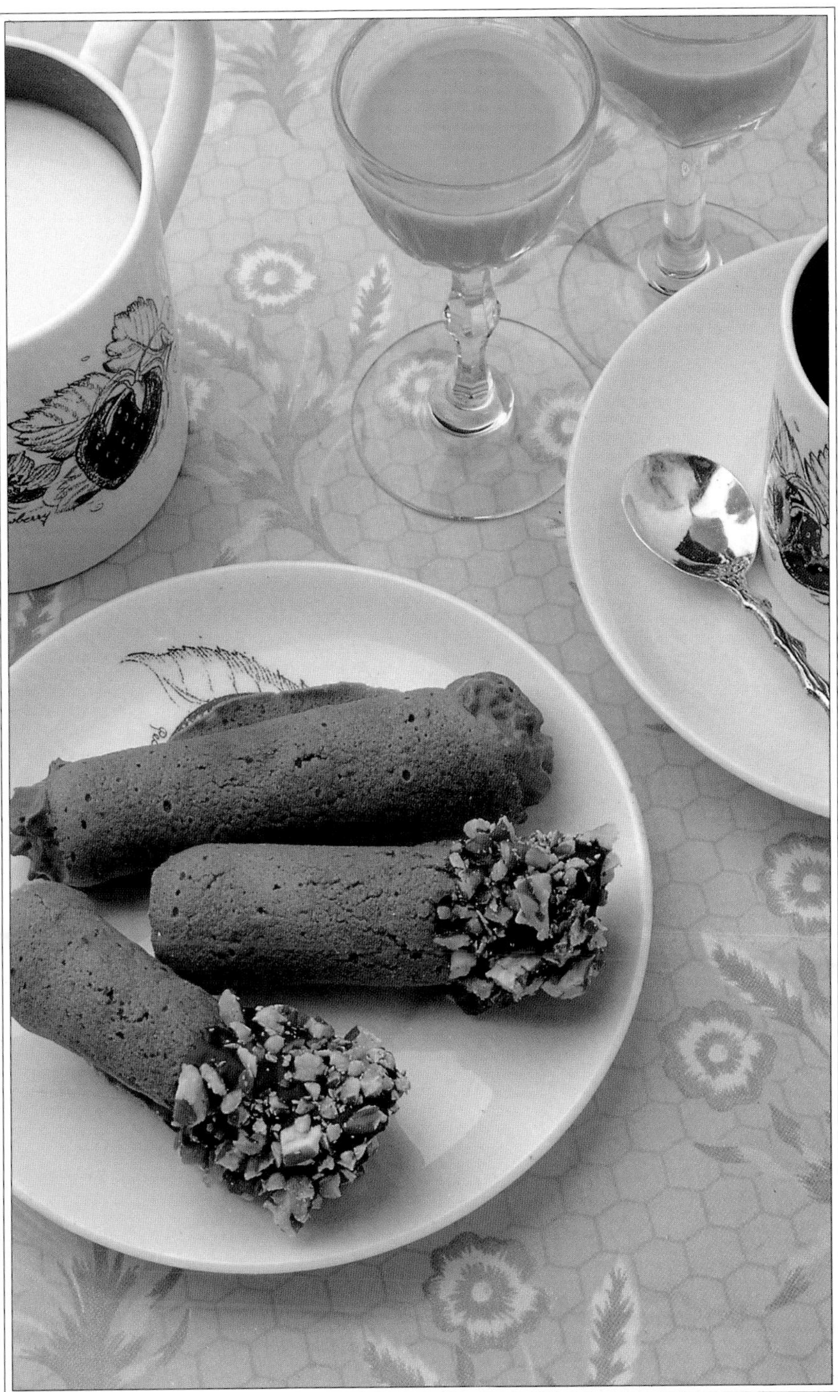

ALTERNATIVE DECORATION

Melt 2 squares (2 oz.) bittersweet or semisweet chocolate in the top of a double boiler. Into a cup, place ⅓ cup chopped and toasted almonds.

If you like, dip one end of each cookie into melted chocolate and then into chopped almonds. Place on waxed paper-lined cookie sheet until set.

CHOCOLATE-CHIP PECAN SHORTBREAD

MAKES 32 WEDGES

This is tender, melt-in-your-mouth shortbread. It is so simple to prepare, but the addition of ground pecans and chocolate chips makes a traditional cookie more sophisticated.

1 cup pecans, toasted and cooled
1¾ cups all-purpose flour
¼ cup cornstarch
½ cup confectioners' sugar
¼ tsp. salt
1 cup (2 sticks) unsalted butter, softened
1 cup semisweet or bittersweet chocolate-chips
1½ squares (1½ oz.) semisweet or bittersweet chocolate, melted for drizzling

Preheat oven to 325°F. In a food processor or blender, process the pecans until fine crumbs form; do not over-process nuts as the oil which is released can begin to form a paste.

Place in a large bowl with flour, cornstarch, sugar and salt. Using a pastry blender or fingertips, cut or rub butter into flour mixture until well blended and mixture is almost creamy; do not let butter melt. Stir in chocolate chips.

Divide dough between 2 very lightly greased 8-in. tart pans or cake pans with removable bottoms and pat or spread evenly into pans. Bake 25 to 35 minutes, or until edges are golden and surface appears slightly puffy. Remove pans to wire rack to cool 2 to 3 minutes.

Remove side of pans and place shortbread on heatproof surface. Cut each shortbread circle into 16 thin wedges; this must be done while shortbread is still hot and soft or it will crumble. Return shortbread wedges on their pan bases to wire rack to cool completely.

With metal spatula, remove shortbread wedges to wire rack, alternating direction of wedges with every other one, wide edge, then pointed end up. Spoon melted chocolate into a small paper cone (see Decorating with Chocolate) and drizzle shortbread wedges evenly with chocolate. Leave chocolate to set. Store shortbread for 1 week in an airtight container.

SWEET SUCCESS

Dough can be blended with hand-held electric mixer at low speed, but do not overwork or baked shortbread may be tough or butter melt. Mixture can be baked in a 9- × 13-in. baking aish and cut into long fingers or squares, but the wedges with the crinkly edges from a tart pan look prettiest.

CHOCOLATE CHIP-GINGER FLORENTINES

MAKES 30

These are chewy candy-type cookies named for the Italian city. This lacy version has lots of chopped ginger and is studded with tiny chocolate chips and glazed.

½ cup heavy cream
¼ cup (½ stick) unsalted butter
½ cup sugar
2 tbsp. honey
1⅔ cups slivered almonds
5 tbsp. all-purpose flour
½ tsp. ground ginger
⅓ cup diced candied orange peel
½ cup diced stem ginger
mini-semisweet chocolate chips for sprinkling
8 squares (8 oz.) bittersweet chocolate, chopped

Preheat oven to 350°F. Lightly grease 2 large nonstick cookie sheets or grease 2 cookie sheets; nonstick cookie sheets are ideal.

In a saucepan over medium heat, stir cream, butter, sugar and honey until sugar dissolves. Bring to a boil, stirring constantly. Remove from heat and stir in almonds, flour and ginger until well blended. Stir in orange peel and diced ginger.

Drop teaspoonsful of mixture, at least 3 ins. apart, onto prepared sheets. Spread each circle as thin as possible with the back of the spoon; dip spoon into water to prevent sticking. Sprinkle each with a few mini chocolate chips.

Bake 8 to 10 minutes, or until edges are golden brown and cookies are bubbling. Do not underbake or cookies will be sticky, but be careful not to overbake as the high sugar and fat content lets them burn easily.

Remove to wire rack to cool for 10 minutes, until firm. Using a metal spatula, carefully remove cookies to wire rack to cool completely.

In top of a double boiler over low heat, melt chocolate, stirring frequently until smooth. Remove top of double boiler from bottom and cool about 5 minutes, stirring occasionally until slightly thickened.

Spread chocolate on flat side of each cookie and place on wire rack, chocolate-side up. Refrigerate 2 to 3 minutes, until set. Using a serrated knife, fork or cake decorating comb, make wavy lines on chocolate layer. Refrigerate 10 to 15 minutes to set completely. (Cookies can be refrigerated in an airtight container for 1 week.)

BRANDIED BROWNIE "TART"

8-10 SERVINGS

This is a classic brownie – dense and chewy, made into a sophisticated dessert by the addition of brandy.

2 squares (2 oz.) unsweetened chocolate, chopped
½ cup (1 stick) unsalted butter
1 cup sugar
2 eggs
2 tbsp. brandy
¼ cup all-purpose flour
⅔ cup pecans or walnuts, chopped and toasted
3 oz. fine-quality white chocolate, chopped into ¼-in. pieces

CHOCOLATE-BRANDY GLAZE
¼ cup whipping cream
4 squares (4 oz.) semisweet or bittersweet chocolate, chopped
2 tbsp. brandy
½ cup pecans

Preheat oven to 325°F. Generously grease a 9-in. tart pan. In a saucepan over low heat, melt chocolate and butter, stirring frequently until smooth. Remove from heat.

Stir in sugar and continue stirring 2 minutes longer, until sugar is dissolved. Beat in eggs and brandy. Stir in flour just until blended. Stir in nuts and chopped chocolate. Pour batter into tart pan, smoothing top evenly.

Bake 18 to 20 minutes, until edges are set and cake tester or toothpick inserted 2 ins. from the side of pan comes out with just a few crumbs attached. Remove to wire rack to cool 30 minutes.

Prepare glaze. In a saucepan over medium heat, bring cream to a boil. Add chocolate all at once, stirring until smooth. Remove from heat; stir in brandy. Cool glaze 30 minutes, until thickened, but spreadable.

Remove side of tart pan and place brownie on wire rack over cookie sheet to catch drips. Using a metal spatula, spread glaze over top of brownie just to edges. Decorate the top with two rows of pecans. Leave to set, then transfer to serving plate and refrigerate 2 to 4 hours, until completely cold.

BRANDIED BROWNIE TART ▶

CHOCOLATE VIENNESE COOKIES

MAKES ABOUT 20

This butter-rich, cocoa-flavored European-style cookie looks stunning when piped into an "S" shape and dipped in dark chocolate.

2¼ cups all-purpose flour
½ cup unsweetened cocoa powder
3 tbsp. cornstarch
1 cup (2 sticks) unsalted butter, softened
½ cup confectioners' sugar, sifted
4 squares (4 oz.) bittersweet or semisweet chocolate, chopped
confectioners' sugar for dusting

Preheat oven to 350°F. Grease 2 large cookie sheets. Into a bowl, sift together flour, cocoa powder and cornstarch.

In another bowl with hand-held electric mixer, beat butter and sugar 2 to 3 minutes, until light and creamy.

Slowly beat in the flour mixture in batches, just until blended.

Spoon dough into a large pastry bag fitted with a large star tip. Pipe about twenty 3-in. fingers or "S" shapes about 2 ins. apart onto cookie sheets.

Bake 15 to 20 minutes, or until set. Remove to wire racks on cookie sheets to cool 15 minutes. Using a metal spatula, remove cookies to wire rack to cool completely.

In the top of a double boiler over low heat, melt chocolate, stirring frequently until smooth. Pour into a bowl. Dip each end of cookie into melted chocolate and place on a waxed paper-lined cookie sheet to set. Cover chocolate-coated ends with a strip of waxed paper or foil and carefully dust the middle with confectioners' sugar. Store in an airtight container.

CHOCOLATE CRACKLE TOPS

MAKES ABOUT 38

These are delicious, fudgy cookies with a texture like a brownie. Once baked, the cookie top cracks and the confectioners' sugar creates a striking contrast to the chocolate interior.

7 squares (7 oz.) bittersweet or semisweet chocolate, chopped
7 tbsp. unsalted butter
⅔ cup superfine sugar
3 eggs
1 tbsp. vanilla extract
1½ cups all-purpose flour
¼ cup unsweetened cocoa powder
½ tsp. baking powder
¼ tsp. salt
1–1½ cups confectioners' sugar for coating

In a saucepan over low heat, melt chocolate and butter, stirring frequently until smooth. Remove from heat. Stir in sugar and continue stirring 2 to 3 minutes, until sugar dissolves. Add eggs, 1 at a time, beating well after each addition, then stir in vanilla.

Into a bowl, sift together flour, cocoa powder, baking powder and salt. Gradually stir into chocolate mixture in batches just until blended. Cover dough and refrigerate 2 to 3 hours or overnight, until dough is cold and holds its shape.

Preheat oven to 325°F. Grease 2 or more large cookie sheets. Place 1 cup confectioners' sugar in a small, deep bowl. Using a small ice-cream scoop, about 1-in. in diameter, or teaspoon, scoop cold dough into small balls.

Between palms of hands, roll dough into 1½-in. balls. Drop balls, 1 at a time, into confectioners' sugar and roll until heavily coated. Remove ball with a slotted spoon and tap against side of bowl to remove excess sugar. Place on cookie sheets 1½-ins. apart. Use more confectioners' sugar as necessary; you may need to recycle cookie sheets.

Bake cookies 10 to 12 minutes, or until top of cookie feels slightly firm when touched with fingertip; do not overbake or cookies will be dry. Remove to wire rack for 2 to 3 minutes, just until set. With a metal spatula, remove cookies to wire rack to cool completely.

SWEET SUCCESS

These cookies are best eaten as fresh as possible as they dry slightly on storage, but they will last for several days in an airtight container. Pack them in single layers so the tops are not damaged.

CHOCOLATE-HAZELNUT PINWHEELS

MAKES ABOUT 60

This two-toned cookie is unusually flavorful. The combination of the light orange-flavored dough and the mocha-hazelnut flavored chocolate works well.

⅓ cup hazelnuts
3 tbsp. unsweetened cocoa powder
1 cup (2 sticks) unsalted butter, softened
¾ cup sugar
1 egg
1 tsp. vanilla extract
finely grated zest of 1 orange or ½ tsp. orange extract
½ tsp. coffee powder, dissolved in 1½ tsp. water

Preheat oven to 350°F. Place hazelnuts on a small cookie sheet and toast 12 to 15 minutes, until golden brown, turning nuts once. Cool slightly. To remove skins, rub the hazelnuts in a clean dish-towel or place in a strainer and rub together. Toss in a coarse strainer to remove the skins.

Place hazelnuts in a food processor fitted with the metal blade and process until coarsely chopped. Add cocoa powder and using *pulse action*, process until nuts are very finely chopped but not oily. Set aside.

With electric mixer, beat butter and sugar 2 to 3 minutes, until light and creamy. Add the egg, vanilla and orange zest and continue beating until well blended and smooth.

Gradually stir in flour and salt, just until blended. Line work surface with large sheet of waxed paper and transfer half the plain cookie dough to waxed paper. Cover with another sheet of waxed paper and roll out dough to an 8- by 11-in. rectangle. Slide onto a large cookie sheet or tray and refrigerate while preparing remaining chocolate dough.

Beat hazelnut-cocoa mixture and dissolved coffee powder into plain dough remaining in bowl, just until well blended and smooth. Place a large sheet of waxed paper on work surface and scrape dough onto paper. Cover with another sheet of waxed paper and roll out to an 8- by 11-in. rectangle.

Remove waxed paper from tops of chocolate and plain doughs. Invert chocolate dough onto plain dough pressing together gently and chill, covered, until slightly firm but flexible, about 15 minutes.

Slide dough onto work surface and remove waxed paper from layers. Trim edges straight. Using waxed paper under the plain dough as a guide and starting from a long edge, roll dough tightly, jelly-roll fashion. Wrap log in waxed paper and freeze at least 1 hour or until firm.

Preheat oven to 350°F. Grease 2 or more cookie sheets. Using a large sharp knife, cut frozen log into ⅛-in. slices and place on cookie sheets about 1 in. apart. Bake 5 to 8 minutes, or until cookies are golden at the edges.

Remove to wire rack 2 to 3 minutes, until set. Using metal spatula, remove cookies to wire rack to cool completely. Cookies will keep in an airtight container for 1 week.

SWEET SUCCESS

This is a refrigerator cookie which can be prepared ahead and baked off as required. Store well wrapped in the refrigerator for several days or in the freezer for several weeks. Slice and bake as required.

WHITE CHOCOLATE FRUIT N' NUT BARS

MAKES ABOUT 20

This bar cookie is jam packed with fruit and nuts. It's sweet and chewy and easy to make and keep – ideal for tailgate parties and children's lunchboxes.

2/3 cup slivered almonds, toasted
1 1/4 cups brazil or hazelnuts, coarsely chopped
1 cup chopped dried apricots
1 cup raisins
1 cup chopped dates
1 1/2 cups shredded coconut
1/3 cup all-purpose flour
8 oz. fine-quality white chocolate, chopped
1/2 cup heavy cream
1/2 cup apricot preserves
1/2 cup honey
1 oz. fine-quality white chocolate for garnish

Preheat oven to 325°F. Grease an 8- by 12-in. baking pan. Line bottom with nonstick parchment paper or foil and grease paper or foil.

In a bowl, combine almonds, brazils, apricots, raisins, dates, coconut and flour.

In a saucepan over low heat, melt chocolate and cream, stirring frequently until smooth. Stir in apricot preserves and honey until well blended. Stir white chocolate mixture into fruit-and-nut mixture and scrape into prepared pan. Spread mixture evenly, smoothing top.

Bake 30 to 35 minutes, until set. Remove to wire rack to cool in pan. Invert onto cookie sheet and remove paper, invert back onto wire rack top-side up. Drizzle with white chocolate and cut into bars.

BLACK-AND-WHITE CHOCOLATE-MINT SANDWICH COOKIES

MAKES ABOUT 20

This is a very upscale version of one of the most popular chocolate sandwich cookies we know. A filling of rich, white chocolate ganache is sandwiched between chocolate cookies; then glazed with dark chocolate.

½ cup (1 stick) unsalted butter, softened
¼ cup sugar
1 egg
1 tsp. mint extract
¼ cup unsweetened cocoa powder
1 cup all-purpose flour

WHITE CHOCOLATE GANACHE FILLING
½ cup whipping cream
6 oz. fine-quality white chocolate, chopped
1 tsp. mint extract

5 squares (5 oz.) bittersweet or semisweet chocolate, chopped
3 tbsp. unsalted butter

With electric mixer, beat butter and sugar until light and creamy, about 3 minutes. Add egg and beat 2 to 3 minutes longer, until mixture is fluffy. Beat in mint extract.

Into a bowl, sift cocoa and flour together. With a wooden spoon, gradually stir into the creamy butter mixture just until blended. Turn out dough onto a piece of plastic wrap and use to flatten dough to a thick disk. Wrap and refrigerate at least 1 hour, or until cold.

Preheat oven to 350°F. Grease and flour 2 large cookie sheets. Remove dough from the refrigerator and divide in half. Refrigerate one half of dough.

On a lightly floured surface, roll out the other half of dough to about ⅛-in. thick. Using a floured heart-shaped or flower-shaped cutter, about 2 ins. in diameter, cut out as many shapes as possible and place the shapes on to prepared cookie sheets; reserve any trimmings. Repeat with second half of dough. Gather up trimmings, roll out as above and cut out as many additional shapes as possible; be sure to have an equal number of shapes.

Bake 7 to 8 minutes, until edges are set; do not overbake as cookies burn easily. Remove to wire racks to cool 10 minutes. With a metal spatula, remove cookies to wire rack to cool completely.

Prepare filling. In a saucepan over medium heat, bring cream to a boil. Remove from heat. Add white chocolate all at once, stirring constantly until smooth. Stir in mint extract and pour into bowl. Cool about 1 hour until firm but not hard.

With hand-held electric mixer, beat white chocolate filling 30 to 45 seconds, until it becomes lighter and fluffier. Spread a little white chocolate filling onto bottom side of 1 cookie and immediately cover it with another cookie, pressing together gently. Repeat with remaining cookies and filling. Refrigerate 30 minutes, or until firm.

In a saucepan over low heat, melt chocolate and butter, stirring frequently until smooth. Remove from heat. Cool 15 minutes until slightly thickened.

Spread a small amount of glaze onto the top of each sandwiched cookie, being careful not to let glaze drip or spread over edges. Chill until glaze is set.

CHUNKY CHOCOLATE BROWNIES WITH FUDGE GLAZE

MAKES 14–16 SERVINGS

A very moist, fudgy brownie filled with chopped pecans and chunks of white chocolate.

9 squares (9 oz.) bittersweet or semisweet chocolate, chopped
1 square (1 oz.) unsweetened chocolate, chopped
½ cup (1 stick) unsalted butter, cut into pieces
½ cup packed brown sugar
¼ cup granulated sugar
2 eggs
1 tbsp. vanilla extract
½ cup all-purpose flour
1 cup pecans or walnuts, chopped and toasted
5 oz. fine-quality white chocolate, chopped into ¼-in. pieces

FUDGY CHOCOLATE GLAZE

6 squares (6 oz.) semisweet or bittersweet chocolate, chopped
4 tbsp. unsalted butter, cut into pieces
2 tbsp. light corn syrup
2 tsp. vanilla extract
1 tsp. instant coffee powder

Preheat oven to 350°F. Invert an 8-in. square baking pan and mold a piece of foil over bottom. Turn pan over and line with molded foil. Lightly grease foil.

In a saucepan over low heat, melt chocolates and butter, stirring frequently until smooth. Remove pan from heat.

Stir in sugars and continue stirring 2 minutes longer, until sugar is dissolved. Beat in eggs and vanilla. Stir in flour until blended. Stir in pecans and chopped chocolate. Pour into pan.

Bake 20 to 25 minutes, until a toothpick or cake tester inserted 2 ins. from center comes out with just a few crumbs attached; do not overbake. Remove to wire rack to cool 30 minutes. Using foil as a guide, remove brownie from pan and cool on rack at least 2 hours.

Prepare glaze. In a saucepan over medium heat, melt the chocolate, butter, corn syrup, vanilla and coffee powder, stirring frequently until smooth. Remove from heat. Refrigerate 1 hour, or until thickened and spreadable.

Invert brownie onto plate and remove foil. Invert back onto rack and slide onto serving plate, top-side up. Using metal spatula, spread a thick layer of glaze over top of brownie just to edges. Refrigerate 1 hour, until set. Cut into squares or bars.

CHUNKY CHOCOLATE BROWNIES WITH FUDGE GLAZE ▶

CHOCOLATE-PECAN MERINGUES

MAKES 22–24

These meringues are hard to describe—somewhere between a cookie and a candy, they were always amongst the Christmas cookies made by my mother's best friend, a real Southern belle and a marvelous baker.

4 egg whites
¼ tsp. cream of tartar
1 cup sugar
2 tsp. vanilla extract
1 cup pecans, chopped and toasted
1 cup semisweet chocolate chips

Preheat oven to 225°F. Line 2 large cookie sheets with foil, shiny side up.

With electric mixer, beat whites and cream of tartar until soft peaks form. Continue beating and begin adding sugar, 1 tbsp. at a time, beating at least 1 minute after each addition; this takes about 15 minutes. Continue beating 4 to 5 more minutes, until whites are very stiff and glossy and sugar is completely dissolved. Beat in vanilla extract. Fold in nuts and chocolate.

Use a tablespoon to scoop up a mounded ball of meringue for each cookie, then use another tablespoon to scrape off onto cookie sheets. Make each meringue with tall, rough peaks to look really spectacular.

Bake 2 hours, turning cookie sheets and reversing top sheet with bottom sheet to ensure even baking. Turn off heat, but leave meringue to dry for 1 hour longer, until completely dry. They should not color too much. Remove meringues from oven and peel each off foil. Meringues can be stored in airtight containers.

SWEET SUCCESS

Do not attempt to make meringues on a humid or rainy day; the meringues will weep.

CHOCOLATE-COCONUT SARAH BERNHARDTS

MAKES ABOUT 16

These delicious, chewy, chocolate cookies are probably called Sarah Bernhardts because they too go over-the-top—except with chocolate! Chocolate-dipped, ganache-topped, chocolate macaroons—there's no more room for any more chocolate.

2 cups shredded coconut
⅓ cup sugar
2 tbsp. all-purpose flour
3 tbsp. unsweetened cocoa powder
1 tsp. vanilla extract
1 tbsp. light corn syrup
2–3 egg whites

GANACHE TOPPING
¾ cup cream
8 squares (8 oz.) bittersweet chocolate, chopped
2 tbsp. unsalted butter, cut into pieces
2 tbsp. shredded coconut

CHOCOLATE GLAZE
6 squares (6 oz.) bittersweet chocolate or semisweet chocolate, chopped
2 tbsp. unsalted butter, cut into pieces
1 tbsp. light corn syrup

Prepare topping. In a medium saucepan over medium heat, bring cream to a boil. Remove from heat. Add chocolate all at once, stirring well until melted and smooth. Beat in butter. Cool, then refrigerate 1 to 2 hours, until thickened and chilled, but not set.

Preheat oven to 325°F. Line a large cookie sheet with foil; grease foil. In a bowl, combine coconut, sugar, flour and cocoa powder. Stir in the vanilla and corn syrup and 2 egg whites; if mixture is too dry, add the third egg white, little by little, until a thick dough-like batter forms and holds together.

Using a miniature ice cream scoop, about 1 in. in diameter, or a teaspoon, place 16 scoops onto cookie sheet. With index finger, flatten each scoop, making a slight indentation in center of each.

Bake 12 to 14 minutes, just until cookies are set on the outside. Do not overbake or the macaroons will be too hard. Cool on cookie sheet 10 to 15 minutes, then remove from foil to wire rack to cool completely.

When topping mixture is cold and thick, beat with an electric mixer 30 to 45 seconds, just until mixture lightens in color and thickens enough to pipe; do not overbeat or mixture will become grainy.

Quickly spoon mixture into a large pastry bag fitted with a ½-in. plain tip and pipe a 1-in. mound on top of each macaroon, pressing tip firmly onto center of each cookie. Chill 1 to 2 hours, until topping is firm.

Prepare glaze. In a small saucepan over low heat, melt chocolate and butter with corn syrup, stirring frequently until smooth. Pour into tall, narrow container, mug or strong paper cup to allow easier dipping. Cool chocolate 10 to 15 minutes.

Holding each macaroon by the very bottom edge, carefully and quickly dip each cookie into chocolate glaze to cover filling and top of each macaroon to within about ¼ in. of bottom, twisting and swirling in chocolate glaze so entire cookie is coated. Leave excess to drip off, then quickly turn upright and place on cookie sheet. Decorate the tops with a sprinkling of coconut. Refrigerate 1 to 2 hours, to set. Remove from the refrigerator 5 to 10 minutes before serving.

COCOA BROWNIES WITH MILK CHOCOLATE-WALNUT TOPPING

12 SERVINGS

This brownie is moist and dense but less fudgy because it uses cocoa instead of chocolate, but still has a dark, brownie-like texture. The milk chocolate-walnut topping is quick and easy to make.

½ cup all-purpose flour
⅓ cup unsweetened cocoa powder
¼ tsp. baking powder
¼ tsp. salt
½ cup (1 stick) unsalted butter
1 cup sugar
2 eggs
2 tsp. vanilla extract
1 cup walnuts, coarsely chopped

MILK CHOCOLATE-WALNUT TOPPING
6–7 oz. milk chocolate
1 cup walnuts, chopped

Preheat oven to 350°F. Grease a 9-in. springform pan or 9-in. cake pan with removable bottom. Into a bowl, sift flour, cocoa powder, baking powder and salt. Set aside.

In medium saucepan over medium heat, melt butter. Stir in sugar and remove from the heat, stirring 2 to 3 minutes to dissolve sugar. Beat in eggs and vanilla. Stir in the flour mixture just until blended; then stir in walnuts. Pour into the prepared pan, smoothing top evenly.

Bake 18 to 24 minutes, until a toothpick or cake tester inserted 2 ins. from the center comes out with just a few crumbs attached; do not overbake or brownie will be dry.

Prepare topping. Break milk chocolate into pieces. As soon as brownie tests done, remove from the oven to a heatproof surface. Quickly place chocolate pieces all over the top of the brownies; do not let chocolate touch side of pan. Return to the oven 20 to 30 seconds.

Remove brownie and, with the back of a spoon, gently spread softened chocolate evenly over the top. Sprinkle walnuts evenly over the top and, with the back of a spoon, gently press them into chocolate. Cool on wire rack 30 minutes.

Refrigerate 1 hour, until set. Run a knife around edge of pan to loosen brownie from edge. Carefully remove side of pan. Cool completely and serve at room temperature.

CREAM CHEESE-MARBLED BROWNIES

15–20 SERVINGS

This is the best of two worlds: a moist, dense brownie marbled with a cream cheese layer – brownie and cheesecake. The contrast in color as well as flavor makes this a great chocolate combination.

6 squares (6 oz.) bittersweet or semisweet chocolate, chopped
3 squares (3 oz.) unsweetened chocolate, chopped
1 cup (2 sticks) unsalted butter, softened
1 cup sugar
½ cup soft brown sugar
3 eggs
1 tbsp. vanilla extract
1 cup all-purpose flour
¼ tsp. salt
2 8-oz. packages cream cheese, softened
⅓ cup sugar
1 egg
1 tsp. vanilla extract
finely grated zest of 1 lemon

Preheat oven to 350°F. Invert a 9- by 13-in. baking pan and mold foil over bottom. Turn pan over and line with foil; leave foil to extend above sides of pan. Grease bottom and sides of foil.

In a saucepan over low heat, melt chocolates and ½ cup (1 stick) butter, stirring frequently until smooth. Remove from heat. Cool to room temperature.

In a bowl using hand-held mixer, beat remaining butter and the sugars until light and creamy, 2 to 3 minutes. Add eggs, 1 at a time, beating well after each addition. Beat in vanilla, then slowly beat in melted chocolate and butter. Stir in the flour and salt just until blended.

In a bowl using hand-held electric mixer, beat cream cheese and sugar until smooth, about 1 minute. Beat in egg, vanilla and lemon zest.

Pour two-thirds of the brownie batter into pan and spread evenly. Pour cream cheese mixture over the brownie layer. Spoon remaining one-third brownie mixture in dollops on top of cream cheese mixture in 2 rows along long side of pan. Using a knife or spoon, swirl brownie batter into the cream cheese batter to create marble effect.

Bake 25 to 35 minutes, or until a toothpick or cake tester inserted 2 ins. from edge of pan comes out with just a few crumbs attached. Remove to wire rack to cool in pan.

When cool, use foil to help lift brownie out of pan. Invert onto another rack or cookie sheet and peel off foil. Invert back onto wire rack and slide onto serving plate. Cut into squares and wrap and refrigerate; or wrap until ready to serve, then cut into squares.

Candies

EASY CHOCOLATE TRUFFLES

CHOCOLATE-COATED RASPBERRY TRUFFLES

MILK CHOCOLATE-PISTACHIO COATED TRUFFLES

CHOCOLATE-STUFFED FIGS AND PRUNES

WHITE CHOCOLATE FUDGE LAYER

CHOCOLATE MINT CRISPS

CHOCOLATE-COATED PECAN TOFFEE

CHOCOLATE FONDUE

CHOCOLATE 'TURTLES'

DOUBLE CHOCOLATE-DIPPED FRUIT

CHOCOLATE-DIPPED CARAMEL APPLES

EASY CHOCOLATE TRUFFLES

MAKES ABOUT 45 SMALL TRUFFLES

Most chocolate truffles are made from chocolate ganache base—chocolate and cream or butter often with the addition of brandy or liqueur as a flavoring. The easiest and most authentic truffles are those irregularly shaped and rolled in cocoa to resemble the real truffle. Truffles can be dipped in chocolate or nuts and the combinations are almost endless; these are easy and foolproof.

⅔ cup whipping cream
9 squares (9 oz.) bittersweet or semisweet chocolate, chopped
2 tbsp. brandy or other liqueur (optional)
cocoa powder for dusting

In a saucepan over low heat, bring cream to a boil. Remove pan from heat. Add chocolate all at once, stirring frequently until smooth. Stir in liqueur if using. Strain into a bowl and cool to room temperature. Refrigerate 1 hour, until thickened and firm.

Line 2 small cookie sheets with foil. Using a melon baller, a 1-in. ice-cream scoop or teaspoon, form mixture into 1-in. balls and place on cookie sheets. Refrigerate 1 to 2 hours, until balls are firm.

Place about ½ cup cocoa powder in a small bowl. Drop each chocolate ball into cocoa and turn with fingers to coat with cocoa. Roll balls between the palms of your hands, dusting with more cocoa if necessary. Do not try to make them perfectly round; they should look slightly irregular. Place on cookie sheet. Add more cocoa to bowl if necessary.

Shake cocoa-coated truffles in a dry strainer to remove excess cocoa, then store, covered, in the refrigerator up to 2 weeks or freeze up to 2 months. Soften 10 minutes at room temperature before serving.

CHOCOLATE-COATED RASPBERRY TRUFFLES

MAKES ABOUT 24

The combination of chocolate and raspberry is perfection and these truffles are a great example of a perfect marriage. They are coated in crisp, dark chocolate, but could be rolled in cocoa powder as in Easy Chocolate Truffles.

10 squares (10 oz.) bittersweet chocolate, chopped
6 tbsp. unsalted butter, cut into pieces
⅓ cup seedless raspberry preserves
2 tbsp. raspberry-flavored liqueur
12 oz. (12 squares) bittersweet chocolate, chopped (for coating)

In a saucepan over low heat melt 10 squares chocolate, butter and preserves, stirring frequently until smooth and well blended. Remove from heat and stir in liqueur. Strain into a bowl and cool. Refrigerate 2 to 3 hours, until firm.

Line a cookie sheet with waxed paper or foil. Using a melon baller, a 1-in. ice-cream scoop or teaspoon, form mixture into balls. Place on cookie sheet and freeze 1 hour, or until very firm.

In the top of a double boiler over low heat, melt remaining chocolate, stirring frequently until smooth; chocolate should be 115°–120°F. Remove from heat and pour into a clean bowl; cool to about 88°F.

Using a fork, dip truffles, 1 at a time, into chocolate, coating completely and tapping fork on edge of bowl to shake off excess. Place on prepared cookie sheet. Refrigerate until chocolate is set, about 1 hour. Store in an airtight container with paper towels covering truffles to collect any moisture up to 2 weeks or 1 month in freezer.

VARIATION

For white chocolate coating, melt 16 squares (1 lb.) white chocolate as directed, but cool to about 84°F before coating truffles. Top each truffle with a candied rose petal or violet. Refrigerate as directed.

MILK CHOCOLATE-PISTACHIO COATED TRUFFLES

MAKES ABOUT 24

This truffle is for the lovers of milk chocolate. The mild, creamy center is coated with dark chocolate, then quickly dipped into chopped pistachios.

½ cup heavy or whipping cream
12 oz. fine-quality milk chocolate, chopped
1 tbsp. unsalted butter
1 tbsp. almond or hazelnut flavor-liqueur
12 squares (12 oz.) bittersweet chocolate, chopped
1 cup shelled and unsalted pistachio nuts, finely chopped

In a medium saucepan over medium heat, bring cream to a boil. Remove from heat. Add chocolate all at once, stirring until melted. Stir in butter and liqueur. Strain into bowl. Refrigerate 1 hour or until firm.

Line a cookie sheet with waxed paper or foil. Using a melon baller, a 1-in. ice-cream scoop or teaspoon, form mixture into balls. Place on cookie sheet and freeze 1 hour, or until very firm.

In the top of a double boiler over low heat, melt chocolate, stirring frequently until smooth; chocolate should be about 115°F–120°F. Remove from heat and pour into a clean bowl; cool to about 88°F.

Place pistachios in a bowl. Using a fork, dip truffles, 1 at a time, into chocolate, coating completely and tapping fork on edge of bowl to shake off excess. Immediately drop into bowl of pistachios and roll to coat chocolate completely. Place on prepared cookie sheet. Refrigerate until set, about 1 hour. Store in an airtight container with paper towels covering truffles to collect any moisture up to 2 weeks or 1 month in the freezer.

SWEET SUCCESS

Truffles can be coated with chocolate only, then drizzled with white or milk chocolate or simply rolled in nuts without chocolate coating.

CHOCOLATE-STUFFED FIGS AND PRUNES

MAKES 24

These little sweetmeats are easy to make and look very pretty if served in little gold candy cases. If figs are unavailable dates would do just as well.

12 large fresh figs
12 extra-large prunes, preferably presoaked or softened
3 tbsp. unsalted butter, softened
½ cup blanched almonds, chopped and toasted
1 egg yolk
1 tbsp. almond-flavor liqueur
3 squares (3 oz.) semisweet chocolate, melted and cooled

CHOCOLATE FOR DIPPING
8 squares (8 oz.) semisweet or bittersweet chocolate, chopped
5 tbsp. unsalted butter, cut into pieces

Using a small knife, remove any remains of the stem of the figs. If necessary, pit prunes the same way. Set aside.

Into a food processor fitted with the metal blade, process butter, almonds, egg yolk and liqueur until creamy. With the machine running, slowly pour in the melted chocolate and process until well blended. Scrape into a bowl and refrigerate about 1 hour, until firm enough to pipe.

Line a cookie sheet with waxed paper. Spoon mixture into small pastry bag fitted with a small plain tip, about ¼-in. Pipe mixture into figs and prunes. Place filled fruits on cookie sheet and chill 30 minutes.

In a saucepan over low heat, melt chocolate and butter, stirring frequently until melted and smooth. Leave to cool to room temperature, about 30 minutes, stirring occasionally.

Insert a toothpick into each filled fruit. Dip each into the melted chocolate and allow excess to drip off. Using another toothpick, push fruit off the inserted toothpick onto the lined cookie sheet. Alternatively, holding stem end, dip filled fruits about two-thirds of the way into the chocolate, leaving one-third of the fruit exposed. Place on cookie sheet. Refrigerate at least 1 hour to set.

Using a thin-bladed knife, remove fruit from cookie sheet to candy cases. Remove from refrigerator about 30 minutes before serving.

SWEET SUCCESS

If you prefer, slice filled figs and prunes crosswise, exposing the filling and arrange on a small serving plate.

WHITE CHOCOLATE FUDGE LAYER

MAKES 36 TRIANGLES

This creamy, white chocolate fudge has a layer of dark chocolate in the middle. It is important to chill each layer before the next if you want a distinct line.

- **1¼ lbs. fine-quality white chocolate, chopped**
- **1 14-oz. can sweetened condensed milk**
- **2 tsp. vanilla extract**
- **1½ tsp. white vinegar or lemon juice**
- **⅛ tsp. salt**
- **1½ cups unsalted macadamia nuts**
- **6 squares (6 oz.) semisweet chocolate, chopped**
- **3 tbsp. unsalted butter, cut into pieces**
- **1 square (1 oz.) semisweet chocolate, melted, for piping**

Line an 8-in. square cake pan with foil. Invert pan. Mold foil over bottom, then turn cake pan right side up and line with foil. Grease bottom and sides of foil. Set aside.

In a saucepan over low heat, melt chocolate with condensed milk, stirring frequently until smooth. Remove from heat and stir in vanilla, vinegar and salt until well blended. Stir in nuts. Spread half of white chocolate mixture in pan. Refrigerate 15 minutes or until firm; keep remaining mixture warm.

In a saucepan over low heat, melt 6 oz. (6 squares) semisweet chocolate and butter, stirring frequently until smooth. Cool slightly; pour over white chocolate layer and refrigerate until firm, about 15 minutes.

If necessary, gently reheat white chocolate mixture and pour over set chocolate layer, smoothing top evenly. Refrigerate 2 to 4 hours, until completely firm.

Using foil as a guide, remove set fudge from pan. With knife, cut into 16 squares. Cut each square diagonally in half, making 36 triangles. Place fudge triangles onto wire rack placed over a cookie sheet to catch drips.

Spoon melted chocolate into small paper cone (see Decorating with Chocolate) and drizzle chocolate over fudge triangles. Store in an airtight container in refrigerator 1 to 2 weeks.

CHOCOLATE MINT CRISPS

MAKES ABOUT 30

These after-dinner-style mints are easy to make, and are an ideal hostess gift. Try replacing the mint with orange for a change.

vegetable oil for greasing
4 tbsp. sugar
¼ cup water
1 tsp. mint extract
8 squares (8 oz.) bittersweet or semisweet chocolate, chopped

Grease a cookie sheet with vegetable oil. Set aside. In a saucepan, bring sugar and water to a boil, swirling pan until sugar dissolves. Boil rapidly until sugar reaches 280°F on a candy thermometer (see "Sweet Success"). Remove pan from heat and stir in mint extract. Pour onto greased cookie sheet and allow to set; do not touch as the sugar syrup is very hot and can cause serious burns.

When mixture is cold, use a rolling pin to break up into pieces. Place pieces into a food processor fitted with the metal blade and process until fine crumbs form; do not overprocess.

Line 2 cookie sheets with waxed paper or foil; grease paper or foil. In the top of a double boiler over low heat, melt chocolate, stirring frequently until smooth. Remove from heat and stir in ground mint mixture.

Using a teaspoon, drop small mounds of mixture onto prepared cookie sheets. Using the back of the spoon, spread into 1-in. circles. Cool, then refrigerate to set, at least 1 hour. Peel off paper and store in airtight containers with waxed paper between each layer. Store in the refrigerator for 1 week.

SWEET SUCCESS

If you do not have a candy thermometer, test the temperature of the boiling sugar by pouring a few drops of syrup into a small bowl of cold water; it should become brittle and snap within 1 minute. Do not touch the brittle sugar until it cools in the water for several seconds.

CHOCOLATE-COATED TOFFEE

MAKES ABOUT 1 ¾ LBS.

This is a very buttery toffee coated with a thick layer of chocolate. Break the pieces into irregular shapes and wrap in cellophane for an attractive gift.

1½ cups pecans (optional)
1 cup (2 sticks) unsalted butter, cut into pieces
1½ cup sugar
¼ tsp. cream of tartar
6 squares (6 oz.) bittersweet or semisweet chocolate, finely chopped

Preheat oven to 350°F. Place pecans, if using, on a small cookie sheet and bake 10 to 12 minutes, until well toasted. Leave to cool, then chop and set aside.

Line a 9-in. square cake pan with foil. Invert pan and mold foil over bottom. Turn pan right side up and line with molded foil. Generously butter bottom and sides of foil.

In a heavy-bottomed saucepan over medium heat, melt butter. Stir in sugar and cream of tartar, stirring until sugar dissolves. Bring mixture to a boil. Cover pan for 2 minutes so steam washes down any sugar crystals which collect on side of pan. Uncover and continue cooking 10 to 12 minutes, or until toffee reaches 310°F on a candy thermometer.

Carefully pour into pan and leave to rest about 1 minute. Sprinkle top of toffee with chocolate and leave 2 minutes until chocolate softens. Using the back of a spoon or a wide-bladed knife, spread chocolate evenly over toffee until smooth. Sprinkle evenly with the chopped pecans if using. Cool to room temperature, then refrigerate until firm and cold.

Using foil as a guide, remove toffee from pan. With the back of a heavy knife or hammer, break toffee into large, irregular pieces. Store in an airtight container for about a week in the refrigerator.

CHOCOLATE COATED TOFFEE ►

CHOCOLATE FONDUE

8 SERVINGS

This is an ideal dessert for real chocolate lovers; the dipping pieces are just a vehicle for tasting the pure flavor of thick, melted chocolate – use the best.

fresh strawberries; seedless grapes; sliced bananas (sprinkled with a little lemon juice); peeled orange segments; fresh pineapple chunks; fresh cherries; cubes of pound cake or angel-food cake; marshmallows
1 cup heavy cream or whipping cream
16 squares (1 lb.) bittersweet or semisweet chocolate, chopped
2 tbsp. brandy or other liqueur

Prepare ingredients for dipping. Wipe or wash fresh fruits and dry well; place on paper towel to absorb any moisture. Cube pieces of cake.

In a saucepan over medium heat, bring cream to a boil. Remove from heat and add the chocolate all at once, stirring until smooth. Stir in liqueur. Transfer to a fondue pot and keep warm.

Arrange fruit and cake pieces attractively on a large serving platter. Furnish each guest with a fondue fork and allow each guest to dip pieces of fruit, cake and marshmallows into warm chocolate.

VARIATION

For a white chocolate fondue, prepare as above but use ⅔ cup heavy cream, 12 oz. fine-quality white chocolate, chopped, and 1–2 tbsp. liqueur. Dip in any variety of fruits and substitute chocolate cake or brownie cubes for pound or angel cake.

CHOCOLATE "TURTLES"

MAKES ABOUT 30

These chocolate-covered nut clusters are an all-time favorite. Use the nuts you like most or a combination, but be sure they are all about the same size.

vegetable oil
Caramel Coating (p106)
3 cups hazelnuts, pecans, walnuts or unsalted peanuts or a combination
12 squares (12 oz.) semisweet chocolate, chopped
2 tbsp. vegetable shortening

Oil 2 cookie sheets with the vegetable oil. Prepare the caramel coating.

When caramel has cooled a few minutes, stir in nuts until they are coated. Using an oiled tablespoon, drop spoonsful of caramel-nut mixture onto prepared cookie sheet, about 1 in. apart. If caramel-nut mixture becomes too hard, reheat over low heat several minutes until softened. Refrigerate until firm and cold.

Using a metal spatula, transfer nut clusters to a wire rack over a cookie sheet to catch drips. In a saucepan over low heat, melt chocolate and shortening, stirring occasionally until smooth; cool chocolate to about 88°F.

Using a tablespoon, spoon chocolate over nut clusters, being sure to coat completely, spreading chocolate over surface. Return drips to saucepan and reheat gently to completely cover all clusters. Leave to set about 2 hours at room temperature. Store in a cool place in an airtight container with foil between layers, but do not refrigerate.

SWEET SUCCESS

When stirring nuts into caramel, stir just until coated. Do not overwork or caramel will crystallize.

DOUBLE CHOCOLATE-DIPPED FRUIT

MAKES ABOUT 12

Just about any kind of fruit can be dipped in chocolate as long as it is dry-dry-dry; even a drop of moisture can cause the melted chocolate to seize and harden. To store chocolate-dipped fruits more than 12 hours, the chocolate should be tempered (see p8). For serving the same day, pure melted chocolate can be used.

about 12 pieces of fruit, such as strawberries; cherries; orange segments; kiwifruit; fresh peeled lychees; Cape gooseberries; pitted prunes; pitted dates; dried apricots; dried pears; nuts
6 oz. fine-quality white chocolate, chopped
3 squares (3 oz.) bittersweet or semisweet chocolate, chopped

Clean and prepare fruits. Wipe strawberries with a soft cloth or brush gently with pastry brush; wash and dry firm skinned fruits such as cherries and grapes. Dry well and set on paper towels to absorb any remaining moisture. Peel or cut any other fruits being used. Dried or candied fruits can also be used.

In the top of a double boiler over low heat, melt white chocolate, stirring frequently until smooth. Remove from heat and cool to tepid, about 84°F, stirring frequently.

Line cookie sheet with waxed paper or foil. Holding fruits by the stem or end and at an angle, dip about two thirds of the fruit into the chocolate. Allow excess to drip off and place on cookie sheet. Continue dipping fruits; if chocolate becomes too thick, set over hot water again briefly to soften slightly. Refrigerate fruits until chocolate sets, about 20 minutes.

In the top of the cleaned double boiler over low heat, melt bittersweet chocolate, stirring frequently until smooth. Remove from heat and cool to just below body temperature, about 88°F.

Remove each white chocolate-coated fruit from cookie sheet and holding each by the stem or end, and at the opposite angle, dip bottom third of each piece into the dark chocolate, creating a chevron effect. Set on cookie sheet. Refrigerate 15 minutes, or until set. Remove from refrigerator 10 to 15 minutes before serving to soften chocolate.

SWEET SUCCESS

If the chocolate is carefully melted and cooled and the fruits kept refrigerated, the chocolate should remain glossy for several hours. This is sufficient for fresh soft fruits such as strawberries and grapes. If you wish to store dipped dried or candied fruits for a longer period, it is better to temper the chocolate, which allows the fruits to be stored several weeks at room temperature (see Cooking with Chocolate).

CHOCOLATE-DIPPED CARAMEL APPLES

MAKES 12

This old fashioned Halloween candy treat takes on a new dimension when coated with rich, dark chocolate. Choose small apples so there is plenty of chocolate and caramel to apple.

vegetable oil
12 small apples, well scrubbed and dried
1 cup pecans, walnuts or hazelnuts, finely chopped and toasted (optional)
6 squares (6 oz.) semisweet chocolate, chopped

CARAMEL COATING
2 1/4 cups heavy cream
1 1/2 cups light corn syrup
3 tbsp. unsalted butter, cut into pieces
1 cup granulated sugar
1/2 cup brown sugar
1/8 tsp. salt
1 tbsp. vanilla extract

Oil a cookie sheet with the vegetable oil. Insert a wooden pop-type stick firmly into the stem end of each apple; do not use metal sticks or small pointed wooden skewers as they could be harmful to children.

In a heavy-bottomed saucepan, stir cream, syrup, butter, sugars and salt. Cook over medium heat, stirring occasionally until sugars dissolve and butter is melted, about 3 minutes. Bring mixture to a boil and cook, stirring frequently, until caramel mixture reaches 240°F (soft-ball stage) on a candy thermometer (see "Sweet Success"), about 20 minutes. Place bottom of saucepan into a pan of cold water to stop cooking or transfer to a small, cold saucepan. Cool to about 220°F; this will take 10 to 15 minutes. Stir in vanilla.

Holding each apple by wooden stick, quickly dip each apple into hot caramel, turning to coat on all sides and covering apple completely. Scrape bottom of apple against edge of saucepan to remove excess; place onto prepared cookie sheet. If necessary, reheat caramel slightly to thin slightly. Leave apples to cool 15 to 20 minutes, until caramel hardens.

If using, place nuts in a bowl. In the top of a double boiler over low heat, melt chocolate, stirring frequently until smooth. Remove from heat. Dip each caramel-coated apple about two-thirds way into chocolate, allowing excess to drip off, then dip into nuts. Return to waxed paper-lined cookie sheet. Leave to set 1 hour, until chocolate hardens.

SWEET SUCCESS

If you do not have a candy thermometer, you can test the temperature of the boiling caramel by pouring a few drops of caramel into a bowl of cold water; it should form into a soft ball when rolled between 2 fingers.

Drinks

CONTINENTAL HOT CHOCOLATE

MAKES 1 CUP

This is the kind of hot chocolate that was served in the early chocolate houses of Europe. It is a bitter-sweet drink that can be substituted for a strong, after-dinner coffee.

1 ½ squares (1 ½ oz.) bittersweet chocolate, chopped
1 ½ tsp. unsweetened cocoa powder
⅛ tsp. salt
½ tsp. sugar
milk

Place chocolate, cocoa powder, salt and sugar in a small saucepan. Using the cup in which the chocolate will be served, fill it about one-quarter full of milk and then add enough water to almost fill cup.

Add the milk and water to the saucepan and, over medium heat, bring to a boil, beating constantly until chocolate is melted and smooth. Boil for 30 seconds longer, beating until foamy, then pour into cup. Serve immediately.

SWEET SUCCESS

Heat the cup by pouring some hot water in it while making the chocolate. Empty and dry the cup before filling with hot chocolate.

FROM TOP RIGHT, CLOCKWISE: CONTINENTAL HOT CHOCOLATE, SPICY HOT COCOA, AND VELVETY HOT CHOCOLATE ►

SPICY HOT COCOA

4 SERVINGS

Hot cocoa is the traditional chocolate drink that always satisfies. It was always waiting for us after sleigh-riding or ice skating, and the smell always brings back childhood memories. I've added some extra spice to this one.

⅓ cup sugar
⅓ cup unsweetened cocoa powder
½ tsp. grated nutmeg
½ tsp. ground cloves
½ tsp. ground ginger
½ cup cold water
1 3-in. cinnamon stick, broken into pieces
1 tsp. vanilla extract
3 ½ cups milk
mini-marshmallows or whipped cream for garnish

In a saucepan, combine sugar, cocoa powder, nutmeg, cloves and ginger. Gradually stir in water until mixture is smooth. Add cinnamon pieces and bring to a boil, stirring constantly. Cook 1 minute longer, stirring constantly.

Gradually beat in milk and bring mixture to below a boil, do not boil, beating constantly until mixture is frothy. Remove from heat, beat in vanilla and strain into large cups or mugs. Top each with a few marshmallows or a dollop of whipped cream.

SWEET SUCCESS

For Minty Hot Chocolate, prepare as above but omit the nutmeg, cloves, ginger, cinnamon and vanilla. After milk is beaten in, beat in 2 tbsp. mint-flavor liqueur or 1 tbsp. mint extract.

VELVETY HOT CHOCOLATE

2 SERVINGS

This is the type of hot chocolate served in the tea rooms of Paris and Vienna. A small pitcher of thick hot, melted chocolate is brought to the table with another pitcher of milk. You dilute the chocolate to taste; then add a little whipped cream—it is heavenly.

4 squares (4 oz.) bittersweet or semisweet chocolate, chopped
3 tbsp. water
2 tbsp. hot water
2 cups milk
whipped cream for garnish

In the top of a double boiler over low heat, melt chocolate and water, stirring frequently until smooth. Remove from heat and beat in hot water, beating until smooth. Pour into a small pitcher or 2 large cups or mugs.

In a saucepan, bring milk to a boil and pour into a separate pitcher, or pour some of the milk into each cup or mug of chocolate. Top with whipped cream and serve immediately.

RICH ICED CHOCOLATE

MAKES 2 TALL DRINKS

This is a wonderful summertime drink: A rich combination of creamy chocolate and espresso coffee served in a tall glass over crushed ice.

1 cup whipping cream
4 squares (4 oz.) bittersweet or semisweet chocolate, chopped
2 tsp. vanilla extract
2 cups freshly brewed espresso coffee, chilled
sugar to taste
grated chocolate for garnish (optional)

In a small saucepan over medium heat, bring cream to a boil. Add chocolate all at once, stirring until smooth. Remove from heat and stir in vanilla. Strain into a bowl. Cool to room temperature. Refrigerate about 1 hour to chill but do not allow chocolate to "set."

To serve, beat cold espresso into the chilled chocolate until well blended and frothy. Fill 2 tall glasses one-quarter full with crushed ice, then pour chocolate-coffee mixture over. Sprinkle with grated chocolate.

SWEET SUCCESS

If you prefer sweetened coffee, add sugar to taste to espresso mixture while it is still hot to be sure sugar is well dissolved.

EXTRA-CHOCOLATE MILK SHAKE

2 SERVINGS

Everyone has their own version or favorite chocolate milk shake – try this for a real chocolate treat.

½ cup unsweetened cocoa powder
½ cup sugar
½ cup water
⅓ cup light corn syrup
1 tsp. vanilla extract
½ cup cold milk
1 tbsp. chocolate-flavor liqueur
1¼ cups chocolate ice cream
grated chocolate

First make the chocolate syrup. In a saucepan over medium heat, combine cocoa and sugar. Gradually stir in water until smooth and well blended. Stir in corn syrup, then bring to a boil, stirring frequently.

Cook 2 to 3 minutes, stirring constantly until mixture is smooth and thickened. Remove from heat and stir in vanilla. Cool slightly.

In a blender or milk-shake machine, combine milk, chocolate syrup and liqueur (if using). Blend 30 seconds. Add ice cream and blend about 45 seconds, just until smooth. Pour into 2 tall glasses and garnish with chocolate curls or grated chocolate.

CHOCOLATE CREAM LIQUEUR

MAKES ABOUT 1 QUART

This creamy, smooth after-dinner drink is surprisingly easy to make.

1 tbsp. instant espresso or coffee powder
¼ cup unsweetened cocoa powder
1 cup milk
1 cup heavy cream
1 14-oz. can condensed milk
1 egg yolk
1 cup Scotch whiskey
⅓ cup light rum
1 tbsp. vanilla extract
1 tbsp. coconut extract

In a large, heavy-bottomed saucepan, combine espresso and cocoa powders. Gradually stir in milk until powders are dissolved. Stir in cream and condensed milk and bring to a boil.

In a bowl, lightly beat egg yolk. Pour about 1 cup hot cream mixture over egg yolk, beating well, then stir cream-and-egg mixture back into the pan. Cook 2 to 3 minutes longer until mixture thickens and coats the back of a spoon. Remove from heat. Stir in whiskey, rum and vanilla and coconut extracts. Strain into a bowl and cool to room temperature, stirring occasionally. Refrigerate 2 to 3 hours until well chilled.

Transfer to a bottle or jar with a tight-fitting lid and store in the refrigerator. Shake before serving.

DELUXE CHOCOLATE EGG NOG

10–12 SERVINGS

This drink is made with raw egg and should be kept refrigerated.

9 squares (9 oz.) bittersweet or semisweet chocolate, chopped
2 cups milk
6 eggs
¼ cup sugar
½ cup brandy or rum
½ cup almond-flavor liqueur
2 tbsp. vanilla extract
2 cups whipping cream
grated chocolate or cocoa powder for garnish

In a saucepan over low heat, melt chocolate and 1 cup milk, stirring frequently until smooth. Remove from heat and stir in remaining cold milk until well blended. Cool to room temperature.

With electric mixer, beat eggs and sugar until pale and thick, 5 to 7 minutes. Gradually beat in cooled chocolate, liqueurs and vanilla.

In another bowl with hand-held electric mixer, beat whipping cream just until soft peaks form. Stir a spoonful of cream into chocolate-egg mixture then fold in remaining cream. Chill.

SWEET SUCCESS

To prepare without alcohol, omit the brandy and liqueur and substitute 1 cup milk, chocolate milk or cream.

FROM TOP, CLOCKWISE: EXTRA-CHOCOLATE MILK SHAKE, CHOCOLATE CREME LIQUER, AND DELUXE CHOCOLATE EGG NOG ▶